T0032717

A YEAR
IN PRACTICE

ALSO BY JACQUELINE SUSKIN

The Collected

Go Ahead & Like It

The Edge of the Continent Volume One: The Forest

The Edge of the Continent Volume Two: The City

Help in the Dark Season: Poems

The Edge of the Continent Volume Three: The Desert

Every Day Is a Poem

Praise for *A Year in Practice*

"If you're looking to get still, turn inward, and learn to trust your voice, this is the book for you. Suskin guides us through a self-inquiry practice that is deeply resonant and beautiful."

Alexandra Elle
New York Times bestselling author of *How We Heal*

"Using the poetry of our lives, *A Year in Practice* shifts our notions of time and space from linear to cyclical. By reshaping time, we can foster acceptance and meaning by working with the seasonal tides and not against them. This book is a grounding force for any creative practice to flourish, however you define it."

Carissa Potter Carlson
artist and founder of People I've Loved

"Filled with soulful poetry and prose, wise creative wisdom, and deeply rooted practices, this book is a balm and a lovingly held container that allows readers to tune both outward and inward in order to create a bridge between ourselves, nature, and creativity. *A Year in Practice* weaves the practical and the unseen in ways that illuminate how we can relate to both the tangible actions and the mystery that hold our creative practices. The tender and unique approach Suskin takes is one that I know will ignite and nurture my own creative practice for years to come."

Lisa Olivera
author of *Already Enough*

"I want every artist to read this book. We're all so exhausted and burnt out from toiling in this digital capitalist hellscape, and Suskin provides the most brilliant solution I've seen: follow the earth's lead. She reverently walks us through the seasons, pointing out the elegant natural order that already exists and how a balanced creative practice is less like a factory and more like a tree. What a relief."

Hallie Bateman
coauthor of *What to Do When I'm Gone*, author of *Directions*

"In her brilliant book *A Year in Practice*, Jacqueline Suskin shows us that creative prompts for artistic expression don't just have to come from within, but in fact start with the earth. This book is a must-read for anyone who wants to feel less resistance in their creative efforts and their day-to-day life."

Marlee Grace
author of *How to Not Always Be Working* and *Getting to Center*

"Through self-inquiry and observation with the support of generative prompts and inspired poems, we are provided an opening, an invitation, and a quiet call of remembrance. Despite a severance from nature due to the demands of capitalism, Suskin asserts that there is a greater rhythm we are asked to fall in step with—a rhythm all living things know. Magic and mysticism are deeply embedded into the very thing we've grown to view as commonplace—the structure and passage of time."

Giselle Buchanan
author of *Incantations* and *Love Letter to Self*,
creator of the Written into Being workshop

A YEAR IN PRACTICE

Seasonal Rituals and
Prompts to Awaken Cycles
of Creative Expression

JACQUELINE SUSKIN

sounds true
BOULDER, COLORADO

Sounds True
Boulder, CO 80306

© 2023 Jacqueline Suskin

Sounds True is a trademark of Sounds True, Inc.
All rights reserved. No part of this book may be used or reproduced
in any manner without written permission from the author(s) and
publisher.

Published 2023

Cover design by Lisa Kerans
Book design by Meredith Jarrett

Printed in the United States of America

BK06727

Library of Congress Cataloging-in-Publication Data

Names: Suskin, Jacqueline, author.
Title: A year in practice : seasonal rituals and prompts to awaken
    cycles of creative expression / Jacqueline Suskin.
Description: Boulder, CO : Sounds True, [2023]
Identifiers: LCCN 2023007934 (print) | LCCN 2023007935 (ebook) |
    ISBN 9781649631343 (trade paperback) | ISBN 9781649631350
    (ebook)
Subjects: LCSH: Creative ability. | Seasons--Psychological aspects.
Classification: LCC BF408 .S875 2023 (print) | LCC BF408 (ebook) |
    DDC 153.3/5--dc23/eng/20230623
LC record available at https://lccn.loc.gov/2023007934
LC ebook record available at https://lccn.loc.
gov/2023007935

Dedicated to the seasons
as I've known them.

CONTENTS

Spring

Summer

All Nature

i.

Oh great city, when this woman
escapes to the forest
she *still* feels the presence
of your weight.

She leaves town
and surrenders to Angeles Crest,
sitting below a giant oak,
stones and acorns in her pockets.

Maybe she is healed by the cleaner air,
maybe she sees a cougar or hears
the call of an owl above Chantry Flat.
Can she understand each omen?

She falls asleep, leaning against the trunk,
and only dreams of darkness.
Then she makes her way back down—
forgetful, recharged, new.

ii.

All of our choices continue to be animal.

Our apartments are like dens

packed close together.

In proximity we need to recall

the rhythmic seasons: summer

for openness, fall for gathering,

winter for solitude, spring for rebirth.

Yet, we forget.

We let our minds take the position

of the North Star, we get used to being

our own guides and miss out

on the wisdom of the inner voice—

Hear the murmur of the planet

beneath all that clatter.

Like a river, like a slow and steady birdsong.

The connection seems to have gone silent,

leaving us with our hard streets

and doors pulled shut.

High tips of buildings

mimicking mountaintops,

persuading us into awe

while we try to brush off a feeling,

an old memory like a spider

or tick behind the ear.

iii.

Whatever we make with our hands

will forever be terrestrial, blood and bone

built into our intellect, particle upon particle

to construct the dirt, the byway,

the apple and the cave.

We will forever be of it, this place,

even as we chip away at its foundation,

even as we long for the hills

where no other humans reside.

Natural rebirth, the city undone

and done again as flesh, as leaf,

or as waves washing away the shore.

Earth will swallow us up.

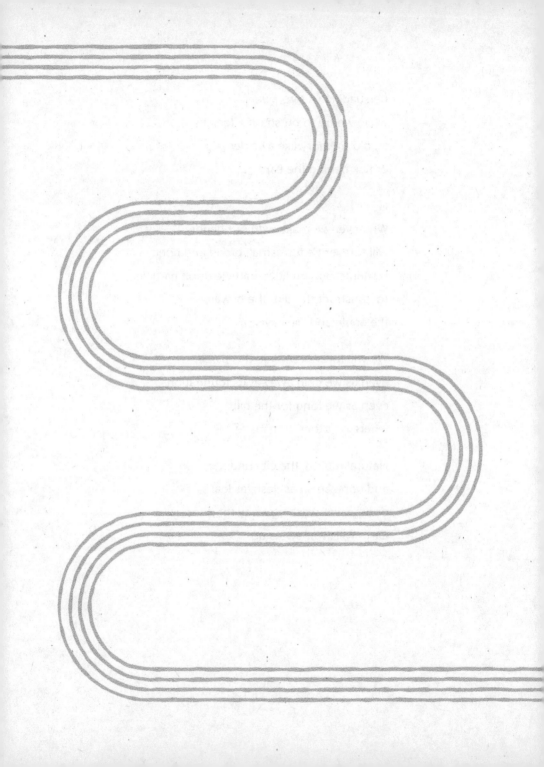

INTRODUCTION

If you picked up this book, if you're drawn to its title and concept, you're likely interested in the intricacies, possibilities, and cycles of creative practice. I'd go so far as to say that you're an artist, but that title doesn't sit well with everyone. It's hard enough to carve out the time in our busy lives to explore our imaginations, let alone give ourselves permission to fully embody our artistic leanings. As fulfilling as it might be to show up for imaginative work in a consistent way, I know it can also be exhausting to fight for an inch of time that allows for the beauty of artistic process, to figure out when and where to be creative, to see the outlets and opportunities to concentrate on expressive methods.

I've dedicated my entire life to artistic practice, and somehow, beyond all odds, the result of this focus is that I get the honor of having a career that invites me to write every day. But I know in the center of my heart that my career is an added gift that supports my process because I'd write every day even if no one paid me to. This is because I'm an artist. This is because I need and want to receive the messages of the universe.

The world we've constructed, the human system we're all part of, the old, silly, and at times horrific structure of our society doesn't often support a framework that highlights the importance of creative practice. But you know, because this book is in your hands, that there must be a way to weave imaginative process into the rhythm of our days. You know that it's crucial we spend time dreaming, crafting, and resting in a state of reverie. Without creative customs or playful applications of explorative whimsy, we'd be entirely without progress.

I yearn to observe and witness the subtle and major details of the world. I crave the tradition of translation and the act of creation. I'm inspired to discover and explore, to expand and grow. I'm compelled to collect and compile my findings, to share them and expose everything that moves me. I can't ignore this innate desire to explain and describe, to express and reveal, to play with this process and enjoy the experience. I see the way ideas bring possibility and revision illuminates perspective. I can't help but want to figure and learn and know more. I understand how healing it is to dig deeper and how transformational it is to reflect upon all aspects of myself and the privilege that is my life.

My practice, in all of its configurations, helps me keep track of time, stay organized, get unstuck, gather material and inspiration, keep clear and grounded, stay healthy and grow, and it gives me the ongoing affirmation I need to continue creating. Creativity brings about personal expansion and cultural transformation. Art-making, like storytelling, poetry, theater, music, filmmaking, drawing, painting, cooking, woodworking, and pottery, helps us remember our capabilities, our origins, our needs, and our responsibilities.

In order to fully embody my devotion to the craft of poetry, I've always needed a rhythm, some guidance to show me the how and when of practice. I'm interested in methodologies that might enrich my process and reveal how I can best express my visions. I've read interviews with some of my favorite artists about their schedules, learning the ways they maintain their discipline and focus. It's really fun to see what works for whom, and it's entirely different for everyone. Each creative person has their own desires, restrictions, style, and pace. At the time I was reading those articles, I began to wonder if I might be missing some information. I felt a deep weariness as I worried about burning out. I was tired from trying to figure out and construct a ceaseless practice on my own. This is when I turned to the seasons for guidance.

As an ecstatic earth worshiper, I tend to look to the planet for instruction in my daily life. Because this place, our only home, offers us everything we need and then some, there's often a perfect answer right below our feet or in the sky above us. I was searching for a creative rhythm to rely on that I didn't have to make up myself, a natural foundation to support me as I prioritized creative practice in my life. After decades of turning my attention to the earth, I began to recognize an essential tempo, a fundamental guidance that showed me when to begin, when to sit down and work, when to share my creations, and when to rest.

In the ongoing effort to better my writing and as I began to closely examine the seasons, I realized how much my practice naturally responds to the rhythm of winter, spring, summer, and fall, and I uncovered a built-in, creative cadence. Over time, I discovered a dependable routine for artistic output that relies on seasonal energy. It isn't something I fabricated; it's something innate that I needed to get back in touch with in order to continue creating my work. Each season is a Muse that evokes a particular artistic possibility if we take note of the instructions offered.

The four seasons are a framework for our experience on earth, and they provide us with phases of creative contraction and expansion and supply us with specific moods and sensations. Each season connects us with our timeline of life. Our memories are aligned with holidays and our bodies with certain types of weather. The seasons directly affect us in so many ways, but overall, it's the character and lesson of each yearly chapter and how each phase influences me that I'm most fascinated with.

As humans, we're caught in a long cycle of forgetfulness. There's so much in our current culture that distracts us from the inherent information the earth provides. We've replaced the cyclical gifts of the seasons with controlled temperatures, ceaseless production schedules, and year-round access to always-ripe fruit. We've cut so many of our roots that connect us with the ebb and flow of earthly process. These changes have brought us comfort and a sense of advancement, but they've also disconnected us from a natural pattern of rest and revitalization.

How are we to conjure up new visions and possibilities for the future if we don't rest when the season says rest? If we don't practice mindfulness when the wild energy of spring shoots through us? If we don't engage in the communal direction of summer? If we don't embrace the preparation of fall? Each chapter of this book serves as a seasonal prompt, an earthly gesture that says now is when you sit still, then let it all rush out, then share it, and then collect the outcomes and loose ends for another round of creative gestation.

This rhythm isn't strictly about the time of year; it's about the spirit that each season evokes. Sometimes I find myself needing to bring elements of summer into my winter state. Sometimes I return to the boosting vibrancy of spring as summer wanes. Humans have always responded to the seasons, as they are our nomadic guideposts, our cues for pace and celebration. These reliable periods offer us a rhythm that is built into our being, and we can access this information anytime we want to get ourselves back on track.

Our bodies, minds, and spirits require the rest of winter. We need the charge of spring in order to reap the bounty of summer. We must engage with the feeling of fall to gather and harvest accordingly. Yet, we often forget the power and importance of the seasons and the way they affect everything in life, including creative practice. The earth gives us consistent prompts, quarterly counsel, and dependable recommendations on a month-by-month basis. It shows us when our creative reserves might wax and wane. We just need to remember to listen and follow its lead.

As artists building our own schedules, we often feel adrift, wondering what to do next and where to put our energy. When I teach, at least one student always asks me how I know when to begin and when to finish a project. "It's intuitive," I say, "but when my intuition feels faint, I turn to the current season and ask for clarity." We can't expect our practice to be high-powered or vibrant all year-round. We, too, are animals following an unseen lead, even when we overlook the formula. For all of our creative desires, there's an obtainable map that leads us to hibernate, to spring forth, congregate, and stockpile.

This book illuminates some of the ways each season requires us to pay attention, showing us the actions it needs us to perform and the practices that fit its specific disposition. Each chapter asks us to remember that we are gifted with a time to begin, a time to ponder, and a time to recharge. By exploring the traditions and motivations of each season, I remember the venerable schedule of the earth and aim to show how each season offers me its own version of this schedule. In one way or another, I continue to reflect, generate, revise, share, and rest. The next season I meditate, write, edit, contribute, and restore myself. After this, I contemplate, engage in creative response, redraft this response, show it to others, and then recharge. Then I deeply consider, I make something of my considerations, I review everything I've examined, I offer it up, and then I relax, breathe, and make room for the next rotation. In short, this book is a guide of remembrance mapped out by the four seasons.

This book is also an exploration of the balance between my personal connection to the planet and my guidance for creative practice after working as a professional poet since 2009. To investigate both sides equally and find the strange and beautiful bridges between them, I had to vacillate freely between body, mind, and spirit. This is a major part of what it is to be an active artist. Above all, this was an open listening process, and although the seasons definitely guided me, I wasn't inflexible or overly strict, and that's my main point here: I don't want you to be either. A framework can be fluid. It's mostly about figuring out how you can give yourself the time and space to be attentive and respond to the intricacies and beauty of life. The rhythm of the seasons wants to remind us that this time and space is naturally built into life on earth.

To be clear, I'm not a master of any of this. I'm a student of the seasons. The practices I discuss in this book are ones I've built over time with some research, but mostly by way of intuitive response, and each one continues to evolve in my life as I read about new methodologies and keep practicing and discovering what works for me. I meditate differently in the winter than I do in the summer. I move differently in the spring than I do in the fall. When something changes, I take note, but I let it change. If there's one thing I'm sure of with creative practice, it's that it doesn't like to be forced, grasped, or squeezed too tightly. It likes to come and go, arrive and fade, lie dormant, and then reveal itself fully once again.

Even during the creation of this book, I found myself fully adjusting my practice. I've never written anything quite like this before, and the way it unfolded, season by season, was a direct result of the fluid exploration I allowed myself to play with throughout the process. I wasn't rigid; there were no rules, but I did try to notice patterns, follow strong hits of intuition, and turn to the seasons whenever I felt stuck. I practiced, I wrote, and I practiced more. I spent a lot of time outside and a lot of time with my nose deep in my collection of poetry books. When I didn't know exactly what came next with this project, I looked to the earth and the special selection of books I've been accumulating for a few decades.

I let myself be drawn to whichever collection called to me, and I flipped through the index in the back, looking for signs of spring, summer, fall, or winter. It was so much fun, like an unusual scavenger hunt—and my word, do poets love to write about the seasons! It felt like a good dose of proof during my process. Artists we love are the most helpful guides, no matter the season, and we can always turn to each other, dead or alive, whenever we're in need. This is one of my favorite things about being a creative person; there's this wildly extensive community of freaks, dreamers, craftspeople, makers, builders, and weavers who left us with their beautiful bounty of work and so much inspiring, accessible information.

Gathering information from the earth is a similar process to my instinctive poem choosing. I just move toward whatever calls to me, whichever flower catches my eye, whatever path looks inviting, whichever scent is the most alluring. Then I let those things give me information. My intuition is my imagination, so if you're wondering whether or not I actually hear messages from the trees, the answer is yes and no. Yes, I give myself time and space to create the voice of the tree as I imagine it singing or whispering or slowly laughing. No, I don't care if I'm just making it up or if the spirit of a tree is truly speaking. That isn't the point, so I don't dwell on it. I just let the earth give me its lessons without overthinking where they come from, and I do my best to translate whatever wisdom lands within me.

With our shifting climate, the seasons are changing, and I recognize that not everyone lives in a place where these transitions are obvious. But as their dependability fades, as winters harshen and summers grow hotter, as rainfall diminishes and the sea levels rise, we continue to live under their ancient structure. As the seasons become less recognizable and more nuanced, it feels even more crucial to follow their lead and adhere to their lessons while we still can. It's less about remembering the weather and more about the flow, the pattern, and the creative tempo. Noticing the intricacy of the seasons wherever you live is akin to tapping into a well of details, subject matter, and lessons that might otherwise go overlooked. This type of observation is always a plus for creative practice.

So, imagine with me for a moment: What happens when we slow down and let the planet tell us when to dive into the depths of the mind, when to relax on the surface, when to share our work, and when to hole up with our brilliant ideas so they can grow steady and safe? Maybe we build something incredible and bring something much needed into fruition. Maybe we mend some major wounds and reconnect with a sense of collective direction. The method of the seasons is available to all, and as this great configuration encourages us, it guides our creative flow and reminds us of all we have access to if only we pay attention, if only we practice accordingly.

No Seasons

The word spreads that our days
all run into one another, only blue skies,
and without night we wouldn't sense a change.
Did you not see the full bloom of pink
along the boulevard, same as last year?
The silk floss trees are heavy
with big pods that split open
and spew white garlands of fluff.
Did you miss those hours of morning fog?
The neighbor's high roof was cloaked.
When it's fall, there is a feeling
in the air that lasts all day and I sit
on my front stoop to warm up in the sun.
When it's winter, it finally rains
and I close the windows, buy chestnuts
by the pound, and bake squash in the oven.
When it's spring, the windows are open
and the whole town goes from burnt color
to vivid green and yellow. When it's summer,
the fans are always on high, I cut cold
grapefruit with my slender knife that Yasmine
brought from France, and I hardly ever
leave my bed but for the ocean.

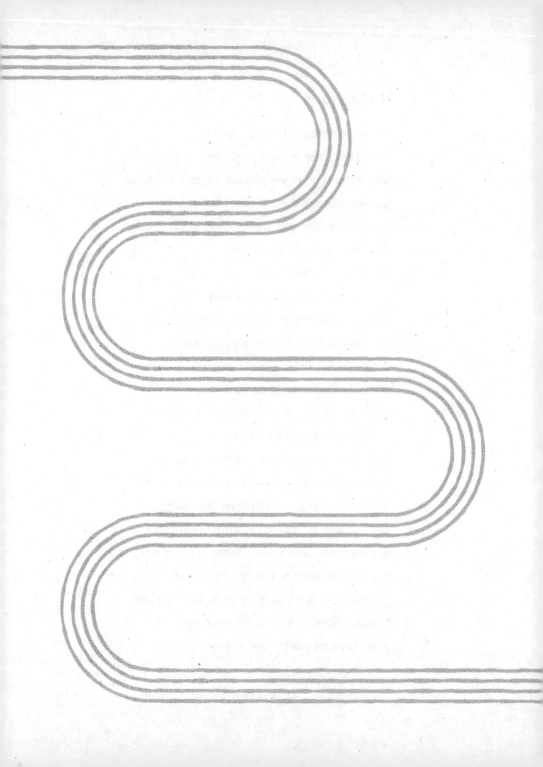

WINTER

Quiet – Contemplative – Solitude – Rest
– Slow – Still – Peaceful – Sluggish – Inward –
Introspection – Pause – Reflection – Withdrawal
– Silence – Focus – Development – Calm –
Restoration – Recharge – Reverie – Dormancy

***

How might one endure the silent
and secluded nature of winter?

Be the bear, enter a deep cave, and
dream, dream, dream.

***

Even though winter can be long, cold, and gray, I deeply appreciate all that it offers my creative practice. It may not always be the most productive time of year in the sense of word counts or project completion, but it's an opportunity for undisturbed contemplation that bolsters the future of my artistic work.

For these cold months, I reassess my intentions, connect with my subconscious, and recharge my imaginative well.

Winter is my time to rest, dream, and get in touch with my sources of inspiration. I find the silence soothing, the hiatus healing, and this tranquility affects the way I approach my artistic desires.

The winter Muse instructs me to refine my visions, study, and clarify my direction, but above all else, the season asks me to restore myself so I can come back to my craft with renewed energy. With the information I gain from my inner exploration, I'm able to move into another phase of creative process with refreshed perspectives and fleshed-out concepts.

The discerning work of winter involves a lot of introspection and uninterrupted time for reflection, so I pause many of my social obligations from late December through February and spend a lot more time at home, at my desk, in my bed, in my bathtub, and on my couch. This season is the gestation period for creativity, the point in the experiment where thoughts start to connect to images, where I find space for expansion and ready myself for the year of action to come.

Think back on previous winters in your life and consider what you've learned. As you notice your personal patterns in this part of the yearly cycle, how do your past experiences inform your life now? What helps you stay grounded throughout the pensive months of winter? Are there specific rituals, celebrations, or traditions that make winter easier or more inspiring for you?

Consider how you'll spend the next few months.

Do you have to travel?

Can you build some retreat time into your schedule?

How can you slow down?

Can you avoid the stress of the holidays in some way?

What restorative foods will you eat?

What will you read that will help you envision your year to come?

In what ways will you put your creativity first?

Is there something specific you'd like to work on?

What will you do for your body during these cold and sluggish months?

As I plan for winter, I focus most on rest and reflection. It's a period of careful invention, an exploration of all that was and will be part of my ongoing creative practice. While the outer world goes quiet, I explore the depths of my inner landscape, looking and listening and indulging in the deliberate spaciousness of the season.

Rest

Imagine all of the life underground
that is waiting for spring.

Envision the resting roots, the sleeping creatures

and everything below the surface
that is paused for the season.

Feel the fullness of this stillness.

Feel the necessity of this calmness.

There is silence here, in every den, in
every inch of cold dirt.

There is silence in your home as well.

Your body needs this pause.

Your mind revels in this quietness.

Winter speaks to you and says:

Rush no longer, put down whatever
you carry, curl up, and rest.

Scan yourself from toe to head and head to toe,

letting yourself unwind, releasing all demands.

Breathe into every inch of your body as
it relaxes into this healing state.

Imagine yourself in a warm cocoon,
wrapped in glowing light,

no need to go anywhere or do anything,
no need for any plan at all.

Return to this place of respite every time you
crave the grace of winter's restful energy.
Remember, everything else is asleep now too.

Give yourself permission to go into
the cave and turn inward.

Although winter is my favorite time for focused creation, the most important practice I engage with all winter long is rest.

When I talk about rest, it's crucial to first recognize the work of Tricia Hersey and The Nap Ministry. Under the threat of capitalism and white supremacy, Hersey highlights the complexity of rest for the Black community and defines it as an act of Black resistance. As I connect with rest in winter, I understand it as a privilege first and foremost and equally pay tribute to it as a political refusal for those who have historically been denied access.

Thankfully, this season commands a stillness, a silence, and a pause that our bodies and minds require in order to show up fully for the vibrant months ahead, no matter who we are or where we're from. Many other animals hibernate during winter. There isn't much in our current systems of culture that reinforces rest, but every year winter does its best to remind us to slow down and get under the covers for a while.

This period of rest doesn't equal a dry spell or a creative lull; on the contrary, it can be a time that overflows with visions and inspiration. There are many ways rest engages with our creative practice. While we allow our bodies and minds the time to restore, we can also balance our days with moments of reflection, research, movement, meditation, and breath. From all of these restorative practices, we uncover realizations, new perspectives, lines of poetry, or song lyrics.

Restful activities often give us just enough renewal so we come out on the other side with a bloom of ideas.

My constant reminder to myself all winter is to not push too hard. The essence of the season reminds me that I don't have to document every aha moment that happens in these cold, quiet months. I don't have to share every discovery or turn every insight into a poem. In the winter, I'm much more inclined to commune with the Divine and let those conversations remain private. I recognize that I don't actually have the energy to turn each spark of innovation into something tangible, and I let myself accept this truth. This is the influence of winter, the way it teaches me to shift from an overly productive participant's pace into a person with a battery that needs to plug in and recharge gradually in order to rise up refreshed for the act of creation.

Rest isn't easy for us, and we have to be intentional about it. I find that it's always helpful to plan for my practice, even if that practice is to rest. Ask yourself what you feel able to accomplish in a day, a week, or a month. Tap into the honest reserve of your energy. What tasks do you feel up to? How will you ensure that rest is a central part of your winter schedule? A lot can be accomplished in these sleepy months of contemplation, but if you position rest as the central focus of your routine, you'll emerge from this season with more endurance for the working days ahead of you.

What does an ideal period of rest look like for you?

Unwinding looks different for everyone, and you'll need to spend some time making a list of ways you can actualize rest in your daily winter life.

Maybe once a week you wake up and immediately take a hot bath. Maybe you watch a movie in the middle of the day. Maybe you get under your electric blanket and read a book for an hour after lunch. Resting usually requires doing (or not doing) something that will break your routine of constant output. How can you convince yourself to pause and be leisurely?

You'll have to choose activities that will force you to slow down. You'll have to remind yourself that resting will expand your creative practice in the long run, even if it seems like the opposite is happening in the moment. Experiment with what works best for you. Sometimes meditation can feel very restful for me, but in other moments, it activates me so deeply that I come out of it with a bounding vibration. In winter, when I'm looking to lean into rest, I like to nap. Sleep feels like the most restorative thing I can do for myself. What form of rest feels right for you?

With any self-reflection, I like to let myself get idealistic before I get practical. Try starting with the finest fantasy of rest, then slowly reel it in to your reality. Maybe pull from past experiences and then balance that with new potential. What can rest look like in your life? What can you adjust to bring this vision into fulfillment?

It can also be helpful for you to clarify what your intentions are for resting. Why do you want to rest? What do you think rest will do for your creative practice? Spend some time with these questions, and don't expect to come up with a quick plan of approach. Actualizing rest will take time, and winter gives you just that: the time to dream up what will fulfill you most.

The examples in this section showcase some of my favorite forms of rest. This might come across as a lot of self-care guidance, but a foundation of rest is what allows me to reap the benefits of winter's creative bounty. It's always important to incorporate rest into creative practice, but in winter I'm genuinely inclined to pause, and my respite feels supported by the season.

I practice many of these self-soothing methods throughout the year, but as I apply them to my winter plan, there's one thing I like to consistently remind myself of: restoration is more important than any other desired outcome.

If I need to stop in the middle of an exercise and sleep or eat, I do it. If I need to pause and write furiously in my notebook after meditating, I do it, but I don't *expect* that kind of inspiration to come. That's the most important part: putting down the demand. I remind myself that my nervous system needs a break, and this period of minimal stimulation is perfect for such repair. I let it all be loose and slow. I let it all be soft and quiet. That's the gift of winter, the reminder to always circle back to rest and reflection, to let the lack of obligations and the tired tone of the season take charge and lead the way.

Prompts from the Planet

What do plants and other animals do in the winter?

They go dormant. Seeds wait, inactive in the dark soil or stored away, safe and dry.

They harden, keep warm, and get slow. Some stop growing. Others sleep and dream.

Below ground, everything works anew, protective and focused on survival.

The plant world pauses its creation and changes its approach, waiting for the sun to return.

Remember, we are part of the same cycle.

Remember to ask yourself: *What is the natural world up to right now? How does it include me? How is it my mirror?*

PRACTICE: Stillness

Stillness is the main mode of winter. The season tells everything to stop. In stillness, I don't ask myself to do anything, think of anything, be anything, or make anything. But from practicing stillness, I usually end up with an abundant offering of visions and designs.

The direction for stillness seems simple: *just be still,* but it can feel much more complex if we haven't engaged with this practice in a while.

Similar to a meditative state, when I invite myself to be still, I'm usually seated or lying down. In my practice, stillness is less formal than meditation, and I can be anywhere as I evoke it. My thoughts can also be a part of it, as long as I'm paused in movement, as long as I'm fixed in place and at ease in my body.

In stillness, I typically notice everything around me that isn't still. I witness the world moving, my senses are heightened, and I enjoy feeling the juxtaposition of my motionless self. I like to let my eyes go out of focus, allow my breath to slow and quiet, and be present but in a very inactive way. I practice staring at the horizon, staring at a single tree, and staring at the sky. I investigate how it feels to actually do nothing, to lose sight of anything specific and delight in the strange relief that follows.

I feel most safe and at ease in this state in my home, but sometimes I'll walk to a park bench after it snows so I can be part of winter's tranquility. I don't usually time myself in stillness; it's more of a momentary embodiment that I invite in throughout the day. This practice helps me find the calm of winter. In other seasons, I'm not as inclined to be still, but in winter, I work it into my days as much as possible as a way of remembering how to pause, as a way of soothing myself and restoring my nervous system. It may seem like there's a lot less going on in winter, but asking myself to notice more minimal movements helps me sharpen my observational skills, which is always good for poetry.

How does it feel to be stationary? You have turned to stone, and yet your breath still moves, your heart still beats. You may be immobile, but there is no actual way to be completely motionless in human form. This part of the practice always thrills me, noticing the activity of my body even as I try my best to remove all animation. I am hushed, I am peaceful, but life never actually stops. There is something comforting about this, like seeing the fish under the thick ice of the lake in January, seemingly frozen but for the smallest flutter of their gills.

This is what stillness inspires: a deep noticing, a refined ability to listen and observe so closely that the world starts to offer up its bounty of infinite details for the artist to wield. Try writing down your thoughts about silence and stillness. See what comes up when you think of yourself leaning into this practice, even if you aren't able to do so fully. A single still moment can offer respite, and that's what I suggest you carve out for yourself during winter.

PRACTICE: Restorative Movement

Even as we assign ourselves with the much-needed pleasure of rest and stillness, our bodies continue to need
tending during this lull. It can be easy to forget to move
in the winter when we want to curl up and read all day,
but forgetting our bodies isn't an option. There are many
restorative movement practices available to us, but I'll only
touch on the surface of what the wellness world has to
offer in this category.

My body is such a crucial player in my creative practice, and during winter, it craves special attention. As
opposed to other times of the year when I'm interested in
building strength or exploring high-energy exercise, winter is the season for slow motion, deep stretching, and
gentle postures.

Think of generating warmth while resting on the floor
or dancing. Find calming music that helps you move your
muscles and get your heart rate up a bit, then find the
floor again. I really love going on walks in the winter. There
aren't many people out and about when the air is frigid or
the snow is falling. Winter walks provide the highest quality of silence and breath for me, and I find this is the perfect
way to incorporate nourishing movement into my practice. Just make sure you move at least once a day because
although you're in the cave doing some deep dozing, you
won't be able to maintain that quality of relaxation without
including your muscles, lungs, and bones. Just rolling your
neck a few times in both directions is helpful.

I usually practice yoga on my own, but during the winter, I seek out teachers. I watch videos and yearn for guidance because it's definitely harder to get moving on my own in the cold. I like the repair postures of yin yoga, with a lot of Child's Pose and stillness in between moves. I like to get my blood flowing in the morning or in the middle of the day. Even the slowest and smallest movement will help fill my body with a hint of liveliness, and this often leads me to my journaling practice. Movement doesn't just restore my physical sense of well-being in the winter, it also ignites some kind of inspiration. As I open my notebook after a long stint of lying on a bolster in a deeply healing posture, I don't try to write something of merit or clarity as much as I simply allow myself to release and flush out my mind. This is what winter tells me to do.

I find my calm as I lean into mending movement. As I stretch, dance, or walk, I gently sift through anything that's building up inside of me without a desire for a coherent outcome. I don't ask myself to put the pieces together or reach a certain goal. Moving my body in the slightest of ways keeps me open and available to winter's reminder that there's nothing I actually need to accomplish. This is my time to heal, contemplate, and relax. Winter supports me in this process, as it's too cold and gray to do much of anything else.

If you're feeling stuck, find a way to move.

If the weight of winter gets you down, restorative movement is your best bet for finding the flow again. Even if your aim is to settle into the finest quality of rest, shifting into this quiet state can be really challenging and bring up a lot of hard feelings. Movement is the way I dig myself out of the emotional snowdrift that winter can sometimes shove me under. If I bundle up and get out of the house, I always move a bit closer to warmth and inspiration. If the gloom of the season starts to affect my mental state, I rely on physical guidance to transform my mood. Even a small practice of stretching or walking around the block can get me unstuck.

If I can't get out of bed because I feel too tired but I also don't want to steep in my slump, I find that doing a body scan is another helpful way to engage with physical information. I start by feeling my feet and moving my attention up through each inch of my body, noticing how my ankles feel, imagining energy flowing through my shins, and by the time I get to my head, I feel much more embodied. I might not get up and write a poem after this; in fact, I might drift back to sleep because this scanning exercise can be very relaxing, but I find that my attitude is attuned whenever I attempt to connect with my body.

ELEMENTAL INSTRUCTION: Water

Water is typically known as the element of winter. Consider this as you move into the depths and the cold. Water freezes in winter, turns into heavy snow, and cycles through the many forms of itself as the season passes. As an element, it's connected to creativity and deep emotion.

Remember, we're made of mostly water, attuned to its patterns and character and guided by its essential presence. Water stores the energy of life's beginnings, and yet, its temperament is phlegmatic.

As you watch water in winter and tune in to its lessons, take note of what resonates with you. Where does this elemental conductor lead you on your winter exploration? See how many ways you can connect with water and its behavior during these dark months. Let it show you how to create your own well of life-force energy. Let it show you how to freeze, stop, and thaw.

PRACTICE: Bathing

The bathtub is one of my favorite places to rest and reflect. In the bath, I practice relaxing my breath; I listen to calming meditations and helpful affirmations; and I sing peaceful songs, cast spells, and record my visualizations. The bathtub gives me the opportunity to privately release myself into hot water for a set amount of time. In the bath I can feel equally engaged and completely lazy. I can take care of my physical well-being, tend to my muscles and bones, and drift into dreamlands all at the same time.

Taking a bath assures a shift in pace. If I feel uneasy about my winter slowness, hard on myself for not getting much done, or feel the inherent absence of motivation that comes with months of lacking sun, the bath comforts me and tells me that all I'm meant to do is unwind. There's no better winter place than the tub for a mind gone blank. The bath cleanses me and gives me the sure sense of repose that I'm always craving in the winter. Saunas give the same effect. Massages, too. Anything that gets you warm and in your body for a set amount of time without a certain objective attached to the experience. I do a lot of face massaging in the winter. I add Epsom salts to my bath. I make sure to close my eyes and let the whole experience take me under its hot, elemental charm.

Make a ritual out of your bath time, but let the purpose be rest and rest alone. Light candles and choose the most tranquil music or relieving podcast. I like listening to Belleruth Naparstek's guided imagery audio series while I soak. Sometimes I watch a show or movie if I want that kind of distraction. I nearly watched the entire *True Blood* series while in the bathtub one winter. It doesn't have to be sacred in material to be sacred in intention. For the period of time that the water is hot, your aim is to recharge yourself in any way you see fit. This is holy. This is worthwhile. This is safe. There is no judgment in the bathtub, so bathing is the perfect practice to circle back to if you end up feeling bad for falling under the winter spell of lethargy.

I often come up with ideas for poems in the bathtub. I also experience a lot of breakthrough healing moments while submerged in bathwater. I've spontaneously created cord-cutting rituals and trauma release ceremonies in the bathtub. These experiences inform so much of my creative work, and because I know this bath space is reliably activating, I keep a journal nearby or record my epiphany rambles into my phone as water sloshes in the background. Here's an example of a poem I wrote based on my bathing experience in Los Angeles.

Only Water Helps

I wake up in the night

and think I hear a woman

singing in the driveway,

her voice an engine.

It's actually a storm,

rare and steady, winter rain.

I drink from the red cup

and place it back

on the charcoal-colored clay saucer.

I get out of bed and start a bath.

I usually feel too guilty

using all of this water

because of the drought.

How else can I submerge and cleanse?

The beach isn't that far away,

but I'm not a crow.

I stand alone

on the back porch, naked

and humming, calling it down.

The water can keep coming if it wants to.

It can turn this dry city into a tangle

of brown rushing rivers, pushing

all of it, all of us, into the ocean.

Bath time can be an incredible offering of clarity, but it can also be a built-in moment for you to completely shut off your brain. Any restful practice has the potential to give you so much creative material, but only if you let it be fluid and free. I love the bath for this reason. The generous gift of hot water provides so much, but it's different every time. Most frequently, it melts me into a state of tranquility, which supports my foremost winter goal of resting on the path toward rejuvenation.

PRACTICE: Sleeping & Dreaming

Sleep may seem like the most obvious form of rest, but it's definitely not the most attainable. So many people have trouble sleeping or don't get enough sleep because of their busy schedules. But this time of year actually tells us to go to bed, and in order to do so, we have to put in some serious effort.

Winter reminds me to prioritize sleep, and I do so as often as possible, which takes careful planning. I build naps into my daily routine during winter more than in any other season. I let myself sleep in as much as I can, and I tune in to the way more sleep affects my quality of life, including my levels of creativity. In winter, I revel in the way sleep revives me, the way it lifts my entire being into a higher place, and I see how this always translates into the caliber of my writing.

Frequent sleep isn't just a method of restoration; it's a conduit for a rich dream life. Dreaming greatly influences my creative work, and the more I sleep, the more likely I am to dream. Not only does my dream life provide me with interesting subject matter for writing, but exploring my subconscious helps me in my healing process as well. When I spend time deciphering my inner world through dreams, interpreting the reoccurring symbolism and evolving scenarios, I better understand my waking life reactions and even witness my overall growth.

Sleeping is inherently an important part of life, but winter gives me a better understanding of what this means. When I sleep more, I'm better able to show up for my creative work, but I'm also better able to resist the constant pull to create. It's a both/and situation. Sleep is both creative and restful. Therefore, during the winter, when sleep seems easier to come by under the groggy nature of cold weather and cloudy skies, I reap all the benefits of the practice and don't feel the pressure to oppose something so natural and necessary.

Whenever you can, gather up your eye masks, weighted blankets, white noise machines, aromatherapy kits, and audio books—whatever tools you need to help you sleep—and start practicing. Sometimes I'll set a timer for ten minutes and I won't necessarily find a deep sleep, but I'll slip into a dream state that refreshes me. This is different from the active posture I use in meditation because I typically put myself to bed and lay on my heating pad, inviting myself to truly rest. Like all other winter practices, this isn't about the pressure of perfection or a desired outcome; it's about trying to show up for rest and seeing what happens as a result.

I let myself sleep longer and longer if I'm able. I recognize what this does for my mind, body, and spirit, and I thank winter for turning me into the bear in the cave. We are allowed to be the bear in the cave, especially during this dark season that is desperately trying to show us we can stop producing and start dreaming.

If all your tricks and tools help you get into a good, deep sleep rhythm where dreams are allowed to transport you, then you can expand the practice and start enriching your dream world. I keep a notebook handy for my dreams. Try writing down your dreams, even if all you can recall is a glimpse. The more you talk about your dreams and write them down, the deeper your exploration can go. I try my best to lucid dream by training myself to notice that I'm asleep while I'm in a dream. Those are the moments when I can make changes to my dream world that lead me deeper into my subconscious. If it interests you, read about this technique and try to bring back information from the astral plane to influence your work. Maybe you're the kind of dreamer who gets in touch with your ancestors while you sleep. Turns out, they have a lot to offer your creative practice. Here is a poem that explores a dream I had while I was retreating in Joshua Tree.

The Whale Dream

We stood along

the edge of the continent,

a large group, maybe

one hundred people.

A whale came to us.

I leaned out over the water

and it put its mouth on my mouth.

The same way the black mustang

did in the desert. Samson, with his

velvet muzzle. Whale with its

lip so smooth, so solid and wet.

Everyone gasped around us.

When it was time for the whale

to retreat, after we exchanged

the ancient feeling, the truth

of connection, it went below

the surface and I followed it.

I jumped in and fell and fell

into the only color that matters,

the deep blue that still holds light.

But I could not become a whale.

Covered in salt, I found my way

back to land, alone.

Winter gives you time to go deeper, sleep harder, delve into your dreams, and do whatever you want to do with the information you discover there, even if that means waking up and doing absolutely nothing. Sleep has a lot to offer you, and now is the ideal time to get as cozy as you can without worrying that you should be at your desk or making plans. If winter is asking you to do anything at all, it's to get comfortable in your dream den and go to sleep. By the time I get to winter, I'm usually exhausted and open to rest, but that doesn't mean it feels right when I first start incorporating it into my practice. Be easy on yourself as you begin to align with the restful techniques that work best for you and recognize how all of this rehabilitation enables you to gain creative clarity.

Reflection

In stillness, we find the ability to listen deeply

to ourselves, the planet, and the many
voices that guide us in our practice.

Winter gives us the spaciousness
to contemplate all angles,

all details of what was, of what brought us to this point,

and now we choose what to muse
on, what to mull over and enrich.

Let yourself be present as you become

the vessel for new images, updated pathways,

versions of the future transforming in your mind's eye.

What you once saw as solid shifts now

because you took the time to give it a different voice.

What you once knew to be your medium expands now

because you assigned it a new name.

This is the height of the experiment, all creative potential

gestating in infinite color, held within
the quiet world of self,

readying for a timely rebirth

according to whatever guidance you conjure.

Do this work with care, at a bear's pace,

below the cover of ice, held

by the soothing silence of snow.

Winter isn't an overarching, magical period of complete and utter pause. We still have to work in the winter, the holidays are stressful and busy, and most of us can't afford to just hop off the wagon of life to enter a warm, restorative den for months on end. But we can attempt to lean into the practice of reflection and prioritize a period of contemplation.

I find there's no better time than winter to look over the creative material I've gathered. This time of year, the conditions are right for me to contemplate all of the experiences, feelings, and musings I've collected throughout the seasons. Along with a great routine of rest, I find the space to navigate my core, survey my inner landscape, and take note of the details that reside within. And because I'm inclined to create more down time for myself, I'm able to be casual and meticulous with this process all at once.

This is a time-consuming undertaking, and it can't be rushed. Under the serene spell of winter, I feel most at ease and most open to the practice of reflection, and with everything in the outside world under a blanket of snow, I feel more aligned to delve into my depths, to bring forth new visions, to reimagine my creative approach and update my routine.

Winter is the time when I'm most frugal with my energy, so nothing about my personal discovery method gets hasty or flooded. This season asks me to flesh out my concepts, look at my inspirations from all angles, and really take the time to visualize, refine, and reconsider. Every winter I end up clarifying which creative projects I want to spend time with during the rest of the year.

Reflection is an essential part of artistic practice, and with the guidance of winter's suspension, I can build my craft with uninterrupted precision that no other time of year so thoroughly illuminates.

Where do you need to be in order to reflect?

It's not always as easy as saying, "Hey, it's winter. I'm ready to reflect." Just as I have to get into the flow of rest, I have to set myself up for the work of reflection. It takes a lot of emotional effort to fully witness myself, even when I know I have the time and space to do so.

To get into a reflective mindset, ask yourself to list some methods that you know help you with this kind of personal review. Is there a tried-and-true tradition that you always use to get yourself into a state of mindfulness? Personally, I like to sit at my altar, stare at a candle, and focus on my breath for at least ten minutes before I start my creative reverie. Maybe there's a time of day that you most enjoy this state of deep pondering. Perhaps you like to walk with a notebook or record yourself speaking aloud while you consider your inner workings. Or maybe you know you need to schedule uninterrupted time alone in order to get into your depths.

Most often it's the setting I choose that helps me begin self-exploration. It's sometimes less about the actual starting practice and more about the amount of time and where I spend it that allows me to feel secure enough to look within. For example, if I'm on a hike in the forest, I can almost immediately tune in to my internal voice, whereas if I'm stationary at home, it might take some breathing or stretching before I can get into the fullness of my rumination.

Do you already know what works best for you? It can be helpful to list out your ideas and see how they align with the following methods I offer for practicing reflection. If you're already in touch with what ritual or environment best carries you into reverie, you might set up shop there and find it easier to apply the examples that move you most.

Reflection is a constant part of creative practice, but over the last fourteen years of my poetry career, I've found that in wintertime I can go further into contemplation with less resistance. That's what the four seasons show us: paths of least resistance and energetic rhythms that already exist for us to learn from and utilize. In winter, I better understand solitude and the way it affects my creativity. When it's cold outside, when the weather says, "Stay home," I find it's much less complicated to allow myself long stretches of meditation and self-consideration. Winter is a time that supports the most careful aspects of my craft, the time-consuming parts that aren't dedicated to final form but to fluid analysis, extensive curiosity, and attentive review.

PRACTICE: Retreat

Although winter instinctively gives us pause, most of us are unable to put our lives on hold for three months to revel in the complete silence of the season. But knowing how important it is to pay attention to this natural phase of slowness, how can you create space for yourself to rest and reflect?

Every year during the winter months, I like to set some time aside to go on retreat. This doesn't mean I leave my home or book some expensive sanctuary in a remote landscape, but it does mean I work the gift of solitude into my daily life as much as possible.

My practice of retreating started the summer I graduated from college, when I accepted an offer to house sit for my friend's parents in Florida, taking care of their animals and garden for three months. This was the longest period I'd ever spent by myself.

After the first two weeks, I found a routine. I'd wake up early and write on the porch, watching the humming-birds drink from the feeders I filled the night before. I'd water the garden, eat lunch, and do more writing at the big dining table that I'd turned into my desk. Then I'd go for a walk, read during the afternoon rains, and write a bit more before bed. I had very few visitors, I danced a lot, and I hardly ever went into town. I wrote my first zine at that dining table. I took LSD for the first time in that forest. I learned about permaculture, I studied soil and butterflies, and I healed my then-broken heart after a difficult breakup.

What was so monumental about that experience was the way it grounded me in my sense of self and provided a deeper understanding of my needs when it comes to my creative practice. Before giving myself this great offering of uninterrupted time, I wasn't aware of how much I needed it in order to tap into my inner world. As an only child, I always valued my time alone, but until that moment, I hadn't fully experienced the way my solitude connected to my artistry and healing. While accessing those quiet depths as a house sitter, I made room for the Muse, I learned my writing rhythm, and I looked into so many unaddressed aspects of my life that required deep, undisturbed processing.

Since that exploratory summer, I've gone on some version of a retreat every year. After some experimenting, I discovered that winter is typically the best time for my solitude. It's easier for me to slip into the space that silence offers when I'm surrounded by the quietness of the season. The following poem exemplifies what I receive from the realm of retreat.

Desert Bear

I know how to heal myself.
In solitude, my routine
of waking up with the sun,
writing, and singing.
To memorize the names of plants.
To walk a familiar gait, softly
as not to disturb the delicate
growth that somehow withstands
wind and heat, day on end.
No one can see me.
I take many deep breaths and never hurry.
I sleep when I feel like sleeping.
What comes out of me in this buoyed state
is the voice of the sacred cosmos.
I hear it start to build
after three days in the desert.
Deep warm sand and cool stone.
They say there is an extensive aquifer
below this landscape, wetness
in the dark. There is a bear who lives
in the boulders. She is me.
Here, she is in her finest season.

I give this example for anyone who is curious about big swaths of alone time and the way this kind of seclusion feeds the artistic spirit, but as I said, I don't need to go away for three months of house-sitting in the woods to land in this nurturing space. In fact, the older I get, the more I need to stay home and balance my responsibilities throughout the seasons. This past winter, knowing that I didn't have the time or resources to retreat in the desert or forest, which are my two top choices for seclusion, I declared that I was on retreat in my own home. After setting up a loose schedule and some boundaries with my partner, I found myself in a very familiar mode of inner focus. I was relieved to implement this practice in my day-to-day life because I didn't actually want to go anywhere, but I knew I needed to root in, reflect, and be with myself.

What does your ideal retreat look like?

Before heading off into seclusion or delving into a home retreat, I suggest dreaming up some sort of framework and creating a potential schedule for yourself, a loose plan and some approximate goals. This way, when you begin your retreat, you'll already have an idea of direction and action.

I like to dream up possible timetables so if I float off into the void after meditating for a long period, I can root myself back into a routine and better utilize whatever time is left in the day.

Make sure you take great care to tend to yourself in the transition from regular life to retreat life. It can be quite startling to go from a busy life of rushed obligations to wide open days of uninterrupted time, and I find it very helpful to have some semblance of a plan to turn to if I feel lost in the freedom that a retreat offers.

Here are some examples so you can get a feel of what I mean before you make your own lists. Remember, these are just illustrations, glimmers of lists pulled from my experience over the years. I'm never too rigid when I'm on retreat or in any other part of my practice because creativity doesn't like rigidity; it prefers to flow like water. Creativity enjoys frameworks like tide charts and moon phases, and it also fluctuates with the seasons and other natural influences. Don't grasp too hard or force yourself to perform or produce beyond your limits, but give your days some shape and make it clear that you have the time and space to daydream and ponder freely.

As you'll see in the example, I sometimes lump my busy work with my creative work because my job is to be an artist, but it may help you to create different categories of focus, like mental health, physical health, paid work, artistic practice, and spiritual practice. These categories will narrow down the things you want to concentrate on and interplay with your intentions around this period of reflection. As you start to envision what's possible, get really dreamy with it and figure out, without too much expectation or attachment, what you might give priority to during this retreat time.

Example Retreat Plans and Categories:

Project List:
- Work on prayer book
- Research for political poems
- Read through my last two journals and transcribe
- Copy and archive loose notes into journals
- Website update
- Outreach for book tour

Process List:
- Process the phone call with Dad
- Do some shadow work around my money beliefs
- Journal about the fears that come up around the new person I'm interested in
- Look over notes from therapy
- Review journals for patterns and lessons I've already learned
- Update affirmations

Schedule Idea #1

6:30am–7am: Wake up, make tea or juice

7am–9am: Altar time, meditation, yoga, journaling

9am–9:30am: Breakfast

10am–12pm: Writing time (with a few short breaks)

12pm–1:30pm: Lunch and a walk

1:30pm–4pm: Writing, reading, research

4pm–5pm: Dinner and a walk

5pm–9:30pm: Reading, writing, dancing

Schedule Idea #2

6am–10am: Wake up, set intentions for the day, breakfast, walk

10am–1pm: Breathwork, journaling, lunch, meditation

1pm–4pm: Creative focus, artistic practice, desk time

4pm–6pm: Movement, body work

6pm–10pm: Dinner, reading, meditation

As you start planning, consider how you can reasonably offer yourself space for winter solitude. What does an idealistic version of a retreat look like for you? How about a practical one? Can you give yourself some retreat space throughout the day—perhaps a quiet morning apart from others or a weekend alone? Even small moments that you set aside can hold the potency of retreat energy if you assign specific boundaries that suit your needs. What do you really desire from this time alone?

Try writing down ten things you can do to pass time in a meaningful way, no matter where you are, and circle back to your list of what it takes for you to find yourself solidly in reflection mode.

This is a time to feel out your creative patterns and note when you enjoy working on your craft, when you just want to sit and think, and when you need to rest and revive. Try documenting these creative practice needs while you have this moment of quiet solitude to support you, then use this insight to steer yourself back into your preferred practice rhythm throughout the year.

If you're feeling stuck, call a creative friend.

Sometimes winter lethargy can translate into a stuckness or stiltedness instead of the restful feeling of tranquility. To shift out of this feeling, I like to call a friend. Winter phone calls can be really illuminating if the person on the other line is also a creative. I like to connect with my artistic friends about the feeling of winter, and inevitably we brainstorm together or collaborate on our approach to practice in the slow season.

Even in solitude, if I'm hitting a wall, I'll pick up the phone. Conversations about art usually evoke the Muse and help me remember why I want to create in the first place. Even if I'm doing my best to rummage through my innermost sanctum, I find that the gift of friendship is always waiting for me, ready to supply me with insight or affirmation. My friends all understand what I'm doing when I'm on retreat in my winter writing cave, so they are that much more available to be there for me whenever I do surface in a moment of need. Winter supports us in our reflection, but our friends are our champions when we drift into the murky quality of gray skies.

PRACTICE: Meditation

Meditation informs my creative work year-round, but the winter months offer such an uncomplicated pause that I'm able to dive much deeper into my seated practice. Many of my poems come from this calm space, as my mind is empty of all the plans and concerns that the other seasons illuminate, and in this restful state, I uncover fertile concepts for future projects.

I'm definitely not a master meditator in any way. Every season I seem to add on to my practice, making adjustments that fit my mood and responding to specific research on methodologies that inspire me. I'm more of a no-mind,

Zen-style student, noticing my breath, doing body scans, and often timing myself for long stints of turning inward and turning off. I often suggest Thich Nhat Hanh's *How to Sit* for folks who are trying to figure out their meditation practice.

By the time I get to winter, my meditation practice has usually waned from my daily routine, so I need to build up my endurance gradually. I start by timing myself in a seated position, with my eyes closed, for five-minute sessions throughout the day, easing back into the space of an empty mind. Then I'll bump the timer up to ten minutes, then twenty, and so forth.

There are countless ways to empty the mind, to delight in the revitalizing practice of noticing thoughts as they pass by, fully witnessing my feelings in my body and sitting with them for as long as I need. One of my favorite ways to meditate is to acknowledge each thought that rises, see it as an image before me, and then watch it dissolve as smoke would in the wind. Over time, this visualization becomes easier and easier, creating a beautiful sweeping display of color and motion as my thoughts continue to come and go. With this practice, I'm able to witness my mind at work while turning back to my breath and releasing attachment to whatever arrives. The feeling of this practice aligns with my breath, and my body can often remember this state of being in daily life, even when I'm not sitting.

This process leads me to the macro questions that I attempt to address through my creative work as a poet. Once I get into a rhythm with meditation, I clear away the rushing, busy thoughts and make room for new viewpoints that I otherwise wouldn't have the space to access. These fresh interpretations enhance my creative work and provide me with rich subject matter.

One winter, I was on retreat alone at a secluded cabin in Northern California. I found myself meditating every day, which I hadn't done in months. So much information was coming to me about the nature of being that I had to sit by the creek every few hours to ground myself. One afternoon, I felt myself circling around an unclear concept and pulled out my tiny notebook to try to give it shape. Here is what I scribbled down while hunched over the cold creek stones:

Life itself is breathing. Life is breathing.

Whatever pattern must play out in a life is the Divine's choice, based on what the Divine is learning. To be an uncarved block of wood is the only way to be—at the mercy of and loved by the Divine design, just being the experiment and the experience of the Divine.

So, what is the "self" and what is the "mind" in this experiment?

It's a way for the Divine to go unnoticed, to get lost and buried, while at the same time noticing itself. As if the mind were created to forget the Divine so the Divine can covertly observe itself in human form, observe its own creation, and view itself at work through the senses. We are a tool of Divine observation. We are the Divine experimenting with its own expansion, a result of mystery and chance. And what is the mind?

The mind is a joke. The mind is a joke that the Divine made for itself, of itself, a reflection pool where it can witness the humor of its own chaos that's taken such strange shape.

I gasped. The mind is a joke! It was as if I'd overturned the last rock and finally discovered a hidden key I always knew was there. These were big thoughts, and only around the space of meditation was I able to attempt to clarify them in my creative writing. I went inside and meditated again. Then I used my rambling journal entry as a prompt, which eventually led to a draft of a poem that I continue to revise. Meditation made room for expansion, and I then came back to my writing practice with more illuminated material. The silent, reflection space of a winter retreat offered this to me.

What are some big ideas you want to expand upon? What do you think the world needs most? If you could put an end to one thing on the planet right now, what would it be? Is there a part of you that feels as if it's locked away? What happens when you consider the word *Divine*?

What feelings or visions arrive after your meditation practice? Try staring at the sky for ten minutes, then writing about the thoughts that pass through you. How can you sit with these things further and creatively reflect back to the world what you uncovered through deep pause and self-reflection?

PRACTICE: Breathwork

Another meditative practice that supplies me with relief and inspiring visions is breathwork. There are many schools of breathwork, and I was introduced to this transformative technique by my two friends, teachers Carly Jo Carson and Lauren Morlock, who both lead sessions online and in person. They each teach their students different forms of rhythmic breathing with musical accompaniment and guide them through the magic of using oxygen as a healing tool.

Breathwork isn't always a restful practice, as it can be immensely activating and bring up a lot of emotion. But in my experience, whatever rises to the surface is something I need to look at; it's material that needs the careful and connected approach that winter provides.

Breathwork can be harmful for people with anxiety or those who are pregnant, so I suggest you research various breathwork methodologies and find the approach that works best for you. Another exercise I practice is box breathing: inhaling for five counts, holding the breath for five counts, and exhaling for five counts. I find this approach to be much gentler than others, and it helps me center myself before I sit down at my desk. In my experience, filling my body with air opens up an incredible passageway to insights I can transfer into my craft. I regularly utilize my creative skills in my personal healing work. For me, the two go hand in hand. Breathwork is powerful any time of year, but I find that my winter practice of reflection aligns well with this technique, giving yet another space and more time for deep introspection that leads to creativity. During one breathwork session with Carly Jo, I uncovered the following poem, writing it in my journal as soon as I surfaced, pulling from what I saw subconsciously while in the world of my breath.

The Eye of Consciousness

We call the moment brutal, tallying death

as we mark history, losing traction, watching

the whole function of the free world loosen

its grip on erratic reality. But consciousness

is an open eye that witnesses everything

without cringing, without blinking, ever aware

and curious. It does not have a body; it floats

through us, the cosmos, taking note. Even now

it stares unfazed, receiving the current

chaos, recognizing familiar devastation.

Awash in the constant rush of information

that will soon again change, it leaves this small

point in time for the next, all past held

in pupil, all knowledge in iris, weightless

and traveling onward with ease.

PRACTICE: Journal Review

My work as a poet has me filling up journals all year long with fragments of ideas. Every time I go on a walk, I bring a tiny notebook. There's a journal in my car, by my bed, and on my desk. I try my best to organize my writing as I go, using little symbols in the margins that tell me when something is a fleshed-out idea, when something requires me to take a closer look, or when something is a weird ramble but also ripe for examination. I know I'll go through these pages at a later date to review and synthesize the clues I left for myself. It's an important part of my process. When I freely write in my journal, which I do in every season, I capture glimpses of information that will later inspire the books I write, but I also have to do the tedious work of looking back through those entries in order to move forward with clarity and purpose.

I like to review my journals during the winter because reflecting on the past can be a severe process, one that takes a lot out of me. The slowness of the season weaves into this work and asks me to be unhurried with my assessment. I set aside blocks of time to sit with a journal or a stack of notes. I transfer ideas that seem solid or important into another journal, and then, after a lot of organizing, I land on a feeling of completion. I love the moment when I've gone through everything from the year and condensed and examined it all to the point where I know I've weeded out the good stuff and can let the rest go. By the end of winter, I've refined my archive, I've reflected on what the year offered me in inspiration and possibility, and I've whittled it all down to things that will be usable for my practice moving forward. After I do this, there's no need to look back again because I'm confident that I've mined everything I'm able to uncover.

As you reflect on your past process, see what treasures you left for your future self. How can you support the inspiring sparks you recorded in your notes? Go through all of your old journals, gather up the ideas that feel worthy of more exploration, and consider what you've left yourself to work with in the coming months. Are there pathways that illuminate specific projects? Are there bits of poems that seem to adhere to a particular theme or thesis? Is there a trail you've left for yourself to follow that explains an array of potential creative results?

After reviewing your notebooks and distilling your thoughts and theories, try coming up with a list of themes, assignments, or goals that will carry you into the coming seasons of creative work. You can get really big with this and make a list of creative projects that you want to complete in your lifetime, or you can keep it small and write down five things you'd like to expand on in the coming year. Which project direction excites you the most? Is there something specific that you could research in order to find clarity and extend this list? Is there a project that's near completion that you'd like to finish?

Winter gives us the opportunity to dig deeper. During this season, we can peel back the layers of our ideas, examine the prospects for new expression, and expand upon whatever inspiration we've collected over the year. By the end of winter, I like to move forward with a potential list of projects I'll concentrate on for the months ahead. This can certainly change as new inspirations or circumstances arise, but having a clear future vision to work with is always a really fulfilling part of the winter process.

How to Prepare for the Work of Journal Review

Imagine yourself seated at a desk in a studio space, garden, or anywhere that allows you to be most aligned with your creative practice. How does it feel to be here? What are you hoping to accomplish in this space? Who are you hoping to accomplish it for? What is the purpose behind the action you're dreaming up in this space? Why do you want to tap into your creativity? Why do you want to draw or paint or make music? Is the outcome based on a concrete goal, or are you more inclined to simply explore and offer yourself reprieve in this space? Sit with all of this and see what comes up.

Figuring out the feelings and reasons behind creative practice can help us see what's most important and understand the type of outcome we're hoping for. Is it a reasonable outcome? Are you giving yourself enough kindness and generosity in the creative realm? I always answer my questions aloud. It's so helpful to hear my own voice as affirmation for all I'm trying to clarify. It's also really advantageous to contemplate in this self-questioning way before trying to gather up all of your creative guidance. Give yourself at least ten minutes for this reflection time and write down anything that feels like a realization.

PRACTICE: Research & Read

After I review my journals, I rest a lot. In this restful reflection, I often go over my list of themes, my possible thesis ideas, the pathways I could take with my writing, and I listen for the Muse as I consider it all. This is usually when I discover the research I need to do to further explore these designs.

Winter is such a perfect time for research. I can casually or fervently follow the trails of inspiration, looking deeper into concepts that I want to elaborate on and trying to find articles and literature that exemplify the spirit of whatever it is that ignited my search.

This is the time of year I do the most reading. This is when I start buying books and wandering internet trails that lead to podcasts or films. I'll give myself a list of books to read during the season, and this collection will reinforce the research I plan to do through the colder months.

I ask myself who has already created work that touches on the themes I'm interested in, and then I explore their creations. Am I pulling from ancient practice? Is this appropriative? How can I align my coming process with my values and still recognize what inspires me? What doesn't work and needs to be reimagined?

Winter is also the perfect time to take an online class. So many practitioners offer great virtual coursework that blends perfectly with research. If there's something you need to study independently, try finding an education source on the internet that you can utilize at your own pace. With fewer distractions, winter is a wonderful period for employing instructional resources. It's also really helpful to bring in experts or other artists so you don't feel like you're balancing this part of the process all on your own.

Research is an endless well, a vagabond with great depth, and winter can hold its meandering nature. I take notes on my notes, I underline and dog-ear, and in this investigation, I discover so much about myself. I see what moves me most, what is hard for me to look at, what confuses me, and what urges me onward. I like the way this practical work blends with my more spiritual introspection. This is when I take the tangible and mix it with the ethereal. This is when everything I pull from my interior landscape joins the collective, when other people's work starts to mix with my personal world, and I find this to be such a natural facet of creative growth.

In the coming months, I'll have my collection of notes and my stack of marked-up books to pull from as I refine my creative undertakings. I'm always grateful for this part of the reflection process, the way I take the components of my past self and begin crafting something sturdy with them for my future self, and the way voices of other artists join me in this process. This isn't the work of completion; it's the bedrock of completion to come, and winter nurtures me while I carefully build it.

Here are a few suggestions to inspire your explorative research:

- For twenty minutes, research something that's been on your mind, then write about it.

- Write about an artist who inspires you.

- Write about an idea you subscribe to that you know you were taught. Question it and see in which ways you follow the rules of the idea and where you stray off on your own.

- Is there a life lesson you continue to learn again and again? Try to write it out.

- What is something that was once very hard for you that is now easier?

- Write a list of your favorite words and what you like about them. Include definitions and synonyms to expand your understanding.

PRACTICE: Editing

If there's one method of winter reflection that requires a bit more exactness, it's the art of editing. It might not seem like editing applies to every medium, but all artists typically redraft and condense their work in some way throughout their process. If I have work that's ready for revision, winter is my favorite time to complete this aspect of organization and refinement.

When I edit my writing, I call upon a very specific Muse who requires me to delve into the intricate definition of each word I choose and tweak them according to my deepest intentions. Who am I writing for? What do I want to inspire in my audience? What has been coming up for me, and how can I deliver this material to the best of my ability? Once you've gathered all of your notes and ideas, editing can feel like the natural next step. It can be a truly magical experience to watch your work take shape under the attentive eye winter provides. Before I edit anything, I get into a meditative state. I sit at my altar and do my best to clear my mind so fresh inspiration can arrive. I find this is the perfect way to call upon the editing Muse.

I also turn to the practice of creative visualization while I edit. I close my eyes, allow an image to float into my mind, then try to connect this image with whatever I'm writing. Bringing in this expansive and imaginative technique, I focus on certain parts of a project or poem that necessitate further explanation and do my best to weave in the visions that rise up. This adds such a richness to my work as I pull from my inner landscape in new and surprising ways. This is especially important if I'm feeling stuck or uncertain of my direction. The practice of creative visualization helps me polish what I'm trying to communicate, adding fresh creativity to something I've potentially been pondering for a while.

For example, one winter, as I contemplated my aloneness, images of a great valley within myself started to appear in my visualization practice. The following poem came from this imaginative work, expanding on the initial notion and improving it until the piece became clear.

The Great Valley of Myself

You retreat and I retreat. I'm not left
with a feeling of need. I recline back
into my own wetness, my own fertile center.
The moon is full and I have a forty-day supply
of pomegranates from the orchard.
I retreat into the great valley of myself.
I pet my own soft locks and delight
in my long-standing harmonies.
Within, I find all the splendor
you'll be missing. Red roots to lick,
an infinite well overflowing with cool,
clear water for me to drink. Here, I accept
a fullness that no other could provide.

Ask yourself if any of the journal concepts you've gathered are ready for your editing eye. Can you engage with this level of preparation that brings you closer to a finished product, or do you need to carefully adjust and tie together loose ends first? Maybe what you uncover isn't anything close to a final edit, but rather the beginning of a practice that will continue in the months ahead. Sometimes I edit a single poem again and again for years. I require a really calm and open mind for this practice. Winter gives me the tranquility to refine my visions in this way and build off of the material I discover during this introspective time.

An Overview of Winter Month by Month

December

Due to the many popular holidays that arise in December, it takes great finesse and planning to hold the solitude of winter sacred during this month. I do my best to travel as little as possible during this time, but I know the holidays are unavoidable for many of us. My advice is to stay connected to your practice to the best of your ability. Can you set aside even small moments of solitude during your family visits? A walk alone with a sketchbook? A short meditation practice in the early morning before anyone else is up? Try to bring something into each day that ties you to your process.

This is the first month of winter, so allow yourself to ease into this slower pace with care. During this moment that really wants us to rest, it's an incredible challenge to exert all of the energy the holidays require, and I like to think of it as my final push, the last exertion before I reduce speed. See how you can balance your understanding of this and prioritize some aspect of repose and relaxation, even in the midst of celebration and togetherness.

Celebrating Winter Solstice

One way I protect my connection to the season is to celebrate the winter solstice, or hibernal solstice, which happens around December 21. This marks the shortest day of the year, the longest night of the year, and in some cultures, the beginning of winter.

I like to celebrate winter solstice with ceremony and ritual acknowledgment of the immense gifts that winter offers. I make an altar to honor snow, solitude, evergreens, and hibernating creatures. I'll make a feast, especially if I'm spending time with friends and family, which helps me balance sharing the moment and honoring my turn toward contemplation. It's a perfect opportunity to set my intentions for this season of focused practice.

January

During January, I settle into the depths of my creative rhythm and turn fully inward without interruption, plans, or the need to go anywhere. This month is the height of my winter experience, when I find myself fully able to give in to the wonder of the season's restoration. Depending on the weather and my holiday experience, I either meet January with enthusiasm and excitement or allow myself to fall into my first moment of true repose.

Celebrating the New Year of the Gregorian Calendar

I celebrate the New Year to mark my transition into solitude and self-reflection. On New Year's Eve, I like to sit by a fire with a notebook to contemplate the year passed and the year to come. It's such a potent moment to create ceremony, and I enjoy the chance to honor what was and what will be. This is when I begin the task of reviewing my journals, often starting a new one on the first day of the year and setting the old ones aside for consideration.

February

February is a month of great pause. It's cold enough to remain deep in the cave, and at this point, I'm familiar enough with my state of respite that I don't even question it. By the end of the month, I might start to consider what it will be like to reanimate, but I don't feel distracted because it's still so clearly winter and I'm devoted to all I'm learning under the heavy cloak of its presence.

Poems for Winter

"If Winter Comes, Can Spring?" – Alvin Aubert

"The Cold" – Wendell Berry

"In the Waiting Room" – Elizabeth Bishop

"Winter Solstice" – Alex Dimitrov

"Winter Poem" – Nikki Giovanni

"Winter Love" – Linda Gregg

"Ice Storm" – Robert Hayden

"Ritual for January 1st" – Mandy Kahn

"The moon rose over the bay. I had a lot of feelings."
– Donika Kelly

"Dark Morning: Snow" – Jane Kenyon

"February Leaving" – Ruth Ellen Kocher

"New Year's Day" – Audre Lorde

"The Cold Before the Moonrise" – W.S. Merwin

"First Snow" and "Cold Poem" – Mary Oliver

"White Dog" – Carl Phillips

"Void Only" – Kenneth Rexroth

"Sunset, December 1993" – Adrienne Rich

"Snow" – Anne Sexton

"i'm going back to Minnesota where sadness makes
 sense" – Danez Smith

"Snowfall" – Mark Strand

How to Transition into Spring

Moving from winter to spring is incredibly hard for me. Going from slow introspection to full-on creation can be really confusing, and it often isn't a quick shift. Spring is known to start and stop, and its erratic energy is jarring as we exit our warm, quiet part of the cycle.

Make sure you take extra-good care of yourself during this transition. Whenever spring seems to withdraw, feel free to call upon another bout of winter practice. Let yourself have one foot in the stillness until the real exposure of spring takes hold. This is the time of year that I'm the most careful with my daily plans. I never push myself into spring with too much force because a frost might come, and that's no time to be all out.

Keep hold of your calm until you feel the sun on your face, and if you're paying attention to the world around you, to the plants and the weather, you'll know when to step fully into the next season, and your creative practice will adjust with you.

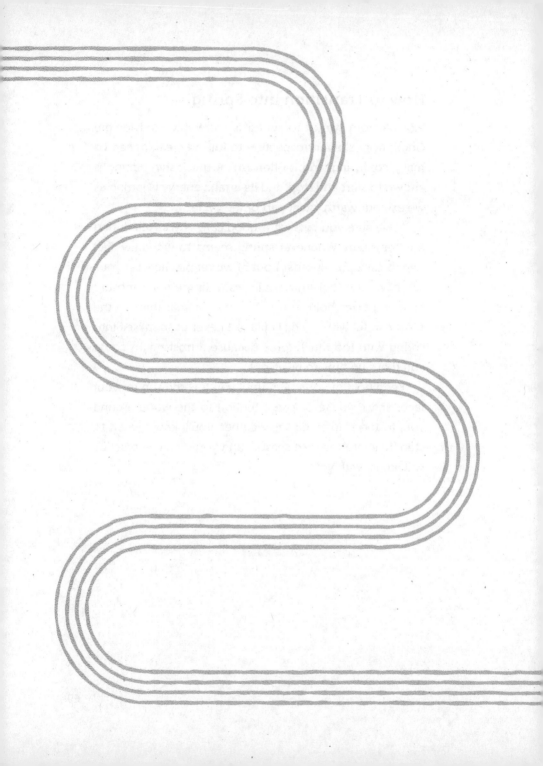

SPRING

Newness – Cleansing – Blooming – Erratic
– Opening – Growth – Exposure – Beginning –
Awakening – Revealing – Hectic – Overflowing
– Vibrant – Reckless – Eager – Unpredictable
– Frantic – Loud – Fertile – Chaotic –
Cacophony – Propagation – Acceleration

***

How best might one ride the wildly
energetic wave of spring?

Go slowly! Don't take too much of
its potent potion all at once!

***

Spring is distinctly alive and overflowing with unmistak-able creativity. This is the season that surges with color and blossom, produces the most exciting achievements from the no-longer-sleeping earth, and brings newness into light after so much darkness. Time itself changes, and the increase of daylight shifts creative output and can affect our artistic moods.

There is a lot to love about spring, but as a creative and highly sensitive person, it's actually my least favorite season when it first begins. Its erratic nature can be difficult to navigate, the way it booms into being and then retreats again, starting and stopping with great force. The transition from the restful contraction of winter is anything but gentle, and I've learned to acutely care for myself in this temperamental time of year. It helps if I break the season into two halves: a slow beginning before a potent unfurling.

As spring returns, I always remind myself that just as the plants are unhurried to emerge, I must be as well. It may seem like the flowers are suddenly in full bloom, but if we take a closer look, we know the buds have been working their way into form for months. Spring is a time of major exposure, when everything that's been tucked away suddenly finds the surface, and the rush of energy that finally materializes is incredibly grand, but the lead up can be jarring and exhausting. In order to rise into the fruition that spring provides, I take the lessons of winter with me and note the ways in which I've stocked up for the wild ride of rebirth that happens every March through May.

The vibrant offering of spring is a crucial catalyst for artistic practice, and only when we harness it with deliberate intention do we reap the benefits. After so much time in stasis, these are the months when we really get back into our bodies, and there is so much information waiting for us in our reenergized movement. With everything around us vibrating at such high intensity, working so hard to grow and survive, we must collect ourselves accordingly and remain grounded as we attempt to actualize the storehouse of visions we developed during winter.

Spring is a time of rigorous balance. It's easy to get overwhelmed and burnt out, so not only must we focus on the magic of emergence and the glorious outcome of creation that follows, but we must also embody the critical heedfulness and discretion that generally accompanies such immense stimulus.

Emergence

All rises from the soil, from seed and darkness.

All aims on high toward newest light.

We follow the extensive reach, expanding from our

hidden realms of quiet contemplation.

All growth is steady, cautious and willing to wait until

frost is put to rest in the past.

We too must let the ebb and flow guide us

in our becoming, still silent while we can be.

Which blossom will be the first to open?

What color will strike the landscape with its fervent gift?

What is our direction in this revival of brightness?

Fortified with deep roots and nutrients, we ask

the sun to provide us with a path.

Reaching toward its vivid voice with our measured

and beautiful offerings, it gives us its timely kiss.

Suddenly exposed, we are fresh again

in form, revealed to the elements, not quite ripe

but on our way to fruition.

Each spring, I remind myself to move into my practice with caution, like a tender animal who hasn't seen the sun in months. Even if I had a bright winter full of passion and I'm ready to bound into action, this feeling of vigilant patience is important for the sustainability of my practice.

After a winter of introspection, I know I have a lot of work to do, and rushing into that work is never a lasting approach. I follow the lead of the season, dipping my toe into the power of emergence and retreating again with the chill in the air, back and forth with great attention to detail until I'm certain spring has fully taken hold. The sun guides me, along with the plants, the birds, and the feeling in my body.

Returning to the working, fervent world often startles me, and shaking off the pace of winter doesn't happen overnight. There are a few days of cold rain, and suddenly the sun's heat arrives. This season begins as a moody, uncertain presence, erratic and unpredictable, charged with a tenacious effort. I always make sure to remain flex-ible when spring starts to show itself in the branches and birdsong. If I'm too quick, I'll end up like the plum tree that put out its blossoms too soon. When a wild storm came out of nowhere, the little flowers got thrashed and the tree's crop wasn't as plentiful. I heed this warning and make sure not to push myself into the mindset of productive out-comes too quickly.

Watch as the bulbs shoot up their sprouts from the dark ground. This magic happens gradually. Then, with just enough anticipation, the buds start forming. And then again, we must be patient for the appearance of the flower. It's the same for our creative practice. Spring is a measured time with influential chapters that offer so much, but we have to move through each stage with patience and attention if we want to receive all it has to offer.

Prompts from the Planet

What do plants and other animals do in the spring? They rise up, slowly at first, and focus on timing.

Seeds send forth roots and careful sprouts. The plant world works within its pattern, with a clear and hopeful aim. Some are too hasty and die in the frost.

Some birds fall from the nest, too quick to try flying.

Remember, we are part of the same cycle.

Remember to ask yourself: *What is the natural world up to right now? How does it include me? How is it my mirror?*

PRACTICE: Patience

The thing I work on most in my life is patience. After years of writing spontaneous poems in two minutes or less, one after the other without pause, I've really had to teach myself the importance of slowing down. Spring gives me the lesson of patience like no other season. Although it's the time of year when we accelerate, I'm reminded every day that nothing grows with intensity all year-round and the cycle is steady, lengthy, and economical.

I turn to the flora and fauna for counsel. No one rushes out from their winter haven too quickly because if they do, all might be lost to a random cold spell. Spring is meticulous, each branch holding on to its buds as long as it needs to, dogged and wise, willing to wait, champions of timing. I learn so much from trying to emulate this resourceful resoluteness, and my creative work thrives when I give it the space and time to become what it needs to become without too much pressure or haste.

Ways to Slow Down:

- Tape a note above your workspace at eye level that says "SLOW."

- Meditate on a single plant that takes its time to grow.

- Create a reasonable pace for your spring projects and return to this as a boundary or grounding point as you get caught up in the glorious rush of the season.

- Let yourself move quickly when you need to, but check in to see if you're bingeing or burning through your energy too hastily.

- Give yourself a lot of time to work on things instead of creating rigorous deadlines. Even if you work well under a deadline, your schedule may not have to be constricting or short in order to give you the helpful feeling of limitation. Continuously ask yourself, *Do I need to rush?* If the answer is yes, spring can help you find the charge to get things done, but see if you can lean into its steadiness so the surge comes in a more consistent way that supports you with longevity.

- Breathe! If I find myself trying to sprint through my practice, I'll pause and breathe to remember I have all the time I need.

- Take a walk. Walking is my most patient place, my favorite way to take a break and return to a healthy pace in my process. Or take a nap. Or just go look out the window. Whatever bit of pause you bring into creative space will not only allow for the patience that discovery requires, but it will also offer room for newness to enter.

Spring doesn't seem like a patient time. Its booming brightness charges at us relentlessly, but within its electric quality is a steady current, an onward force with a specific purpose that hinges on an outcome. Even though we are so excited to finally open our windows and let the fresh air in, we don't want to do it too soon. This time of year reminds me that I'll never get to a place of completion if I run relentlessly with the buzz on the surface. If I practice tuning in to the consistent undertone, the piece of the season that offers fulfillment has a chance to become brighter and stronger.

PRACTICE: Cultivating Outward Awareness

As we come out of winter, our rich season of introspection, spring offers us the time to start turning outward. As with all aspects of practice, each phase is gradual, and so as the days get brighter and the buds start opening, we too begin to open and notice more of the intricacies of the outer world.

Moving from the practice of collecting inner details to gathering outer details gets me most aligned with the feeling of spring. I begin by going to the park or community garden and witnessing the changes that happen over the weeks—all of the plants preparing for their fullest forms, the tiny starts of green, and the hints of purple and yellow that mix with the limey brilliance of the new grass. I try not to go overboard with my creative response when I soak all of this up; I just focus on training myself to tune back into the exterior components that speak to me. Each detail wakes me up from my slumber as I make myself available for this new method of activation.

You can begin to turn on your outward awareness by going outside and walking through the warming world. Take in the changing neighborhood trees, discover the shifting beauty of your yard, venture to a local green space, pay attention to puddles, or stand on your stoop and stare at the sky. However you want to do it, just go outside. The best way to shift from experiencing the quality of your inner landscape is to experience the exterior landscape where you live.

Where can you go to witness the beauty of spring as it takes shape? Is there a place you've missed all winter long? Is there somewhere that's not yet crowded with people but still allows you to expand your experience a bit? While you're there, check in with how you feel. This practice can mimic stillness in a way, but remember that spring is anything but still. Make lists of what is alive around you. What flowers dot the hillside, which ones burst out of the sidewalk first, and what trees are slowest to make leaves? Are your neighbors starting to poke their heads out? Are you wanting to travel? Where would you go right now if you could go anywhere in the world? What are you specifically craving as the season opens up?

This is our return to the art of observing the world around us, not just the world within us. As we tend to our awareness and let it spread to the external, we build a bridge between all we've perceived in our solitude and everything and everyone outside of it. When I see how much is waking up along with me, I feel the beginning of the pull toward interaction, the desire to share my insights and discoveries. This pull comes along with the first jolts of spring's enthusiastic personality. I tread lightly as I open up, and I do my best not to get ahead of myself, to simply put one foot in front of the other, notice what I notice, and enjoy the invigorating feeling of reanimation.

Spring

I began to think in poems last night.
I needed to sleep the city off.
The desert sucks the body dry. The word dry
repeats itself again and again.
At 8:30am it's both cool and warm.
The wind is a good friend.
I've never been here in May before
and every plant I've known for years is new.
This one, usually a dull rust color
is now green with yellow flowers.
There's a different cadence
to the day. When does the house
get hot? When is the best time
for walking? I'm not delicate here.
I'm awake and tuned, as I rub
the seed pods of creosote
between my fingers. In the light
of day, I have no fear.

If you're feeling stuck, tune in to exposure and vulnerability.

As spring begins, I try not to underestimate the impact of the severe exposure that comes with it. I ask myself to recognize how I can best enjoy its fitful energy. After a few months of being unseen, I think of spring as the period that will ready me for the communal joys of summer. It's not just a return to the expansive cadence of creative output, but also a return to more frequent interaction and performance. It's a substantial process to fully rediscover the surface, and the feeling of this great reveal can be damaging like a flood if I don't create a safe rhythm to secure my steady unveiling.

Consider how different it is to be vulnerable in solitude versus around others. How can we gear up to share the discoveries we've uncovered in our self-reflection? Examine how this works for you, one small step at a time.

We don't necessarily think about the intense vulnerability of spring, but after coming out of winter's seclusion, we're suddenly jolted into action, our newness abruptly revealed to everyone and everything. At the same time, we're surrounded by the intensity of the earth as it strives for survival.

This action of rising into the light from the dark season can be rough, especially if you're a sensitive person like I am. In spring, I practice utilizing this vulnerability and choosing my confidants wisely. As the season begins, I select a trusted friend or two and plan to share my project ideas with them. We'll gather together and show each other what we've been brewing up in the cold months.

This is like the first sprout breaking through the topsoil. How does it feel to let someone else in on the intimate ideas that winter guarded so well? The emotions that come up usually indicate whether or not I'm ready to dive in full force or if I need a bit more incubation time.

Be careful who you share your work with as you slowly return to the world of community. Listen to your body as you try to find a balance between the wonderful surge of creative possibility and the tender truth of what it means to express all that's been so private.

To shift into openness, I ask myself grounding questions in order to gather some clarity and intention before moving outward. Try answering some of the following questions for yourself as you begin the process of inviting in the many energies of spring.

- What is the most vulnerable act you can imagine?

- What is your current relationship to the idea of self-care? Why do you think that is?

- What pieces of your winter exploration feel the most tender?

- What are you most excited to show your audience or creative cohorts?

- Can you pinpoint areas where you're holding back, some ideas you thought you'd be excited to share and now feel shy about?

- What are some things you're rigid about regarding your creative practice?

- Think about what you're most afraid of. Now write down the opposite of these fears as an affirmative inverse: *I am not afraid to be loved, I am not afraid to make money, I am not afraid of the ocean, etc.* Make as long of a list as you need and see how it feels to adjust your approach to fear. Try reading these aloud.

- Imagine a voice that speaks to you as you tune in to the outer world. What does it say?

- What is something you have clarity about right now?

ELEMENTAL INSTRUCTION: Air

Air is widely considered the element of spring. Think about this as you move into this season of vulnerability. Wind brings change, it rapidly shifts direction, and it can be very uncomfortable to deal with.

As an element, it's connected to the mind—our thoughts and swirling ideas. Remember how the wind transforms the landscape quickly, how it whips and adjusts the world with its harsh precision.

As you connect with the winds of spring, recognize where this element lands in your experience. Is it hard to deal with this unpredictable movement, or do you like the way it wipes the slate clean for newness? How can you protect yourself from its harshness while also respecting its cleansing presence?

Wood is also commonly associated with spring. With its strength and flexibility, this element connects to the robust mood of the season, the way everything garners its power and bends according to the inherent design of growth that spring inspires. How can we channel the vibrant guidance of wood? How can we adapt and develop our practice in these months of intensity and resilience?

PRACTICE: Grounding Movement

As spring gets underway, I find myself returning to my body. It's not that I forgot about my body during the winter months, but I'm certainly not as inspired to move when it's cold outside. As I begin waking up from head to toe, my connection to movement starts to materialize in different ways.

This is the time of year when I like to build a more dedicated stretching routine. I make sure I dance and get my heart rate up at least three times a week. I go on hikes and take note of the way the earth is changing. I heighten my senses and experience the full offering of spring in color and scent. I start swimming in the cold water, which is my favorite way to reconnect with embodiment. Winter is a very cerebral time, and spring offers a return to the carnal.

So much of the season's newfound exposure resonates in my physical form, and I gain a lot of information for my creative practice by paying attention to these somatic messages. My body is often my best guide when it comes to making the decision to shift my pace. I can feel it in my bones and muscles when the first unsteady part of spring finally starts to display some semblance of balance. I go from resisting movement to desiring more tangible inter- actions with the world. I start with walking because it's the gentlest commencement, but by the time the weather evens out, I'm on my bike or in the river as much as possible.

Spring is a very exciting time for art-making, but it requires a wellspring of wellness and dedication in order for it to serve as a catalyst for fruition. I find so much of my inspiration comes into clarity as my body and mind begin to correspond more. Try writing about this relationship between your body and mind as they gradually revive. We each have our own body-mind connection, and the way this responds to the seasonal shifts is unique for each per- son. It'll take some close observation and a period of trial and error for you to find your physical and mental rhythm as it relates to the energy of spring.

Suggestions on How to Reconnect with Movement

- Mentally scan your body and write about the parts that speak to you the most today.

- Can you feel a blockage anywhere in your body that relates to your creative practice? Perhaps when you sit down at your desk, go to paint, or envision a certain project?

- What does an ideal movement routine look like for you?

- Describe what pleasure is for you.

- Make a list of all the ways you like to move and see if you can utilize one of these modalities each day, even if just for ten minutes.

- Does it help you to move before, during, or after you engage with your creative practice? Why do you think that is?

- My favorite grounding movements happen outside when I'm not wearing shoes and my feet are directly on the earth. Is it possible for you to stand on the earth barefoot? Can you dance somewhere outside? Maybe you can practice yoga in the sunshine? Even simply taking my shoes off and standing in the yard helps me get back in my body after winter.

PRACTICE: Rebirth

Spring is also the time of year when we shed all that we no longer need, letting our newness take hold while we leave behind that which does not serve us.

You've reviewed and refined your reveries all winter long, and now, you're ready to be reborn with a full bounty to work with as the season begins to bloom. Every year spring returns, and with it comes rejuvenation within a complex system of rebirth. We are part of that and so is our creative practice. I like to meet spring by letting myself know that I'm indeed ready for this next phase, I've hibernated properly, and my reserves are fully charged. To give myself a deeper understanding of this and to let the universe know I'm ready to get down to business, I like to make myself clear in ceremony.

There are many ways to be reborn, but when it comes to this transition period of the artistic process, I like to consider my dedication in mind, body, and spirit.

For my creative mind, I'm fond of taking stock and making some promises to myself. When spring begins, I sometimes make an altar of flowers that symbolically connect to the essence of what I hope to achieve in the coming months. Good growth represented by roses, completion embodied in lilac blooms—the symbols of this fresh world align with my dedication to my personal practice. I write down the names of the books I'll write and place them in the center. When my altar is set, I'll shift into the practice of putting my bulletin board in order, organizing all of my winter research, and making a map for myself to follow as I commit to the work ahead.

For my body, I get my studio ready and desk in order. This is the place where I feel safe, where I settle in and lose myself a bit, and if I'm physically comfortable here, my mind and spirit follow.

Then I connect with my spirit and choose when to begin. I won't start working until everything is in its place. Just as I prepare my garden beds for healthy propagation, my studio surroundings set the tone for my creative rebirth.

This is spring cleaning, a cleansing time of arrangement, and it makes sense to pay attention to the details as I set my intentions for the months ahead. Once I'm settled in with my lists taped up and my calendar numbered, I feel ready to join the bursting vibration of spring.

- How can you get ready for your rebirth?

- Maybe you'd like to choose a number of words to write every day?

- Maybe you have an album you'd like to finish writing by a certain month?

- How can you make this orderliness sacred?

- Can you create a ceremony around setting everything up?

My bulletin board is my creative altar. What does yours look like? Can you build up protective energy around this moment and dedicate yourself to some semblance of a schedule for the months ahead? This is when the outline takes shape from all of your reflection time. This is when the plan for creation starts to move forward, and I find that honoring it with my full attention nurtures the possibility for its future form.

PRACTICE: Remembering the Darkness in the Light

Although winter is an obvious season of death and decay, it's important to remember that there's an element of elimination in spring as well. When planting the garden, I learn which seeds are viable, which starts are strong enough to take root, and which varieties are resilient enough to make it through a heat wave.

Spring carries a lot of death with it. I find countless baby birds lifeless on the sidewalk, their new parents not yet wise enough to make a nest in a proper location. I've seen earthworms drown in the rainstorms. Tubers rot, insects infest, and sometimes it's just an off year and a tree doesn't produce as much as it did in the past. I note all of this as it relates to my creative practice as well.

- How does spring relate to your pain?

- What hardships are you carrying with you into this time of year?

- Can you connect them with the darker parts of the season and use that metaphor to help carry your heavy feelings?

- How can spring support you in your discomfort?

- How are you inspired by the death that is equally present in this season of rebirth?

- Can you collect a list of death and creation details as you practice noticing everything spring teaches?

- Do you find you'd rather ignore the more gruesome aspects of spring, or does it feel better to face them?

When it comes to subject matter, spring doesn't force us to craft cheery and life-affirming material. We can lean into darkness even when the light is blaring because death is part of the cycle of life no matter where we are on the wheel. This season of growth is relentless and sometimes it's a churning mess of enlightenment that takes months to parcel out. During this time, I remind myself to never overlook the broken and sad parts of spring. Life doesn't just unfurl into beauty without its rough edges, and as creative makers, it's our job to combine and comment on all sides of the experience.

The Chosen One

Three fledgling sparrows
fell on the front steps this spring.
Their parents made a poor choice,
building a nest on the vertical lattice.
I tried to put them back, made a hot
water bottle and tucked them
into the hanging plants.
They were stone in the morning.

I smashed two black widows on my porch.
Should I have trapped them
and released them in the datura
so that they'd crawl right back?
Yes, that would have been fine.
Killing is never the best choice.

It feels like death is at my door now.
I perform a protective prayer,
a ceremony under the full moon.
I light a candle on each step, ask
for forgiveness, vow to never
kill a spider again and invite the birds
to make home elsewhere.

The next day, a living animal arrives.
An omen on the stoop. Small cat, black
and white, perfect inkblot on his back.
He scoped the entire block, each willing
person at a time, and then chose me as family.

I cast safeguard spells over
the length of his body, a veil
of stars to conceal him from coyotes,
a mantra of magic to let him survive
the street. He is my gift to defend,
my mortal reminder, my sudden child.
Each time he wanders out into the night
I accept that might be the end.

What gracious balance, the light
and the dark, this example showing up
to say: life swings back and forth
in its rising rhythm, resting and then
reviving, coming and going as it likes.

If you're feeling stuck, work with plants.

Plants are my favorite guides in this time of emergence. I'm no herbalist or flora expert; I just love to listen to the green, growing earth, and spring is a very talkative time for plants. There are so many ways to work with the ancient medicine of plants that I can't even begin to scratch the surface.

But plants are always present, freely offering their knowledge and examples. I follow their lead, the obvious nature of growth that bellows during this season, the way nothing is untouched by the frantic tug toward sun, water, and proliferation. Plants help me establish my pace, and they inspire me to create because that's all they do. They just sit steady in the seasonal cycles and respond accordingly.

How can you invite plants into your practice? I put vases on my desk with flowers I cut on walks around the neighborhood. If there's an aromatic bush blooming, I put its petals in my bath. I take tinctures and flower essences, I tend to houseplants and work in gardens, and I study the rich lore of the plant family, relishing in how much the world of vegetation has to offer.

Datura

The first time I read the shamanic
records of Carlos Castaneda,
I notice the small velvet sprouts
show up in the planter beside my window.
Where did the first seed come from?
Did a raven deliver it?
Did the contents of a chapter conjure it?
By the time I finish the book
it's a full-grown plant, white
trumpets and spiked pods, long
arms reaching toward concrete, roots
pushing at the brick barrier. In awe
of its arrival I shake my head and study
the silky leaves. Here is magic
in a form I can touch, mystery
to pet and nurture, the manifestation
of myth sprung from page to soil.
Some say it's poison, but they lack
the recipe for an ancient journey.
I feed it my healthy blood each month.
I shield it from the neighbor's shears.
Oh to be chosen by the sacred source!
A piece of turquoise to guard it
and I'm on my knees under
the full moon, staring as it grows.

Waking up to the fever of spring is made so much easier when explained and exemplified by the emerging colors and patience of plants. Each one has a plan of action, and it doesn't need to be overly complicated for it to work well. We can follow the same strategy with our creative efforts. Don't try to achieve too many things. What are you able to devote yourself to? What type of schedule can you carve out for your artistic pursuits? Will you wake with the sun and set to your grounding movement, or will you use first light to ignite your artwork and follow it up by caring for your body?

Plants remind me that there is a clear balance between making beauty and tending to the source itself. What does the vine need in order to make its flower? This is the time of year when we scatter our seeds, when our food starts to take root, when we build out our rich and fertile beds that will give us so much for months to come. It's the same with creative growth. Spring is when we sow the seeds we stared at all winter long so they can fully form into everything we so carefully envisioned.

How can you tap into this metaphor for your practice? What are you planting now? What will all of this accumulation of contemplative effort provide for your creative journey ahead? Try to weave the vibration of spring into your workspace and see how plants can help you with this planning period. Let yourself get imaginative with it. We are, after all, set to be surrounded by explosions of vivid color, sweet scents, and baskets full of ripe fruit. Why not prepare for the bounty of all this beauty by expanding your connection to it and letting it teach you?

The Overgrown Cul-de-sac

Variegated leaves, long trunk,

spiked bark, fruit pit, wild tuber.

Willingness to marry

the simplicity of sun, to drink water,

to renew by fire and eat up air.

Mindless mystics, show us

the wisdom of waiting

and reaching

as you devour the hillside

in a gesture of vines.

Seeds floating off

to keep the cycle

in succession, roots

rupturing rock to get

to the aquifer, never

taking too much, life

braiding limitless life.

A Few Considerations for Connecting with Plants

- Has a plant ever spoken to you? What did it say? Choose a specific plant as your guide today and observe it with each of your senses. See what it can teach you or how it aids your imagination. Every flower has so much lore attached. Do your research and figure out if there's a specific blossom that suits you for this period of renewal. Take a flower essence or a tincture made from this plant. Drink an herbal tea blend that supports your current creative journey. There are so many ways to get in touch with and learn from the plants around you. Their advice is aligned with the surge of spring and they always help me connect to its rhythm.

- Can you remember the first time you realized food grows from the earth? Write about it.

- Watch a single tree as spring begins and note how long it takes the leaves to reveal themselves. What does this inspire in you? Can you revel in the patience and pace of the tree?

- Is it possible for you to grow anything at your home? Even if it's just a single seed in a pot, the wonder of plant growth can add so much to the creative process, and having a plant that you're personally taking care of enriches the relationship.

- Get involved with a community garden program! I can't emphasize enough how much the world of plants illuminates and energizes my artistic practice. If you can get into the flow of springtime planting, you'll further understand the way our innovation naturally weaves in and out with seasonal cycles.

- Name all of the ways you yourself are like a flower, plant, or tree. This can help you connect to different aspects of your own growth and creative cycle.

- Plants have to break through the soil, the seed membrane, and the bud's shell in order to become whole and fully grown. What do you need to break through in order to continue with your process of creative expression?

Fruition

The season takes hold and moves toward full form,

all visions risen from darkness, everything

on the surface now for all to see.

Praise the glorious flowers unfolded.

Praise the spirited gifts revealed.

Nothing remains closed, all cleansed

and born into this perfected plan,

the place of fulfilment, where each dream

becomes ripe, where every desire

is meant to materialize.

It takes focus to accomplish the story of creation.

Which achievement will find its finish?

Which bright idea will mature in wholeness?

Primed like violet and primrose, no longer awash

in our rumination but ready for felicity, for completion,

for the implementation of choice.

There are two significant parts of spring that clearly guide us in our practice. In the first half, as everything begins to emerge, we take note of our direction and make a gentle plan of action. We slowly wake up, coming back into our bodies and our active process. By the second half, there's enough impetus to start bringing our designs into fruition.

This is an exciting moment, beyond the weird start and stop of weather, past the questioning and crafting of schedules and routes. This is when we buckle down and see our imaginations ushered into the tangible world. This is when we start to accelerate. As the flowers fully open, so do we. As pollen gives its gifts to the world, we too bring our creative magic into reality.

There's so much information offered in the feverish rush of spring. No wonder poets write endlessly about this season! Everywhere you look, there is something to fill you with awe, lust, passion, and beauty. The fervent well is endless, and the source is available to all! It's a very special time of year that feels like a big payoff, and it's this payoff that we carry into summer. In the next section, I'll discuss how to utilize the charge of spring as it transitions from frantic freshness into actual fullness.

PRACTICE: Tangible Manifestation

It can be thoroughly enjoyable to ride the wild waves of spring, follow the lead of plants, and unfold and refold with the changes of weather. As open as I am to going with the flow, I make sure to note when the season actually takes hold and I try to harness the energy instead of slipping into listlessness. Sometimes I have to fight for this moment of recognition, especially as the seasons become less and less reliable with climate change, but I know that if I want to create anything tangible from my long period of contemplation during winter, I have to seize this vibrant energy while it's here.

When I plan to manifest my ideas into tangible form, it takes the energy of spring to see which ones will germinate. Which book do I really want to focus on writing? Which essay calls to me most? What threads seem like they're ready to blend together into a fully formed weave? Sometimes I have to start work on three different projects at once in order to understand which one will truly take the lead. That's the thing about spring: not every seed is usable. It isn't clear what will flourish and what will turn out to be stunted. Everything roars with life and charges onward willingly, hopefully, and if we want to utilize this energy to bring something into the tangible world, we have to follow the rush of it all with our eyes open, wholly uncertain of the outcome.

Making something tangible could be as simple as typing up the many poems you have in your journal, printing them, and making a homemade zine to mail to your friends and family. It could mean stretching a roll of canvas to calculate how many paintings you can make from it or simply picking out your color palette. It could mean finishing a single sculpture or applying for a grant. It doesn't need to be overly ambitious in order to move from your mind into a physical state. But this is your moment to make your choice and begin moving toward some form of completion.

Draw Who You Want

Tonight, I discover that if I draw
a creature in the sand, it will appear.
I kneel and trace a dragonfly
and one flies by. I try the jackrabbit,
usually more elusive, and a slender one
walks out onto the path ahead of me.
It comes closer and circles.
I scribble the grasshopper
and one the color of white granite
lands on my bare knee. I sit before
my altar of quartz and hold
my breath in belief. Who else
do I want to see? I decide
not to draw the snake today.
Not the coyote. But the tortoise.
So rare. A test I suppose.
I forget to draw an eye
and think that means I'll see
a dead one. Walking home I spot
the smallest flare below
a creosote, a strange flower
in the sand. I bend over
and pluck it up only to gasp
in awe at the mummified foot
of a tortoise, whole, waiting for me
as I asked it to be.

A Note on Distraction

With spring comes distraction. How do we restart our practice when all we want to do is go outside and enjoy the new feeling in the air or retreat into the last remnants of our winter caves? This is when I start yearning for socializing, seeing shows, and hanging out with people again. But I'm careful not to overdo it. Spring is my return to diligence when it comes to dealing with distraction. In winter, I let myself off the hook, but once spring roots in, I know it's time to accept the work of fruition. This usually takes some rehearsal. I have to show myself that I can do it, that I'm able to arrive each day for my practice, and that there's enough charge in me to at least try, even if I'm not always productive. I also have to say no to friends and family sometimes, even though I'm all charged up and ready to be out in public. There's a specific balance required during this potent time. If I don't temper myself socially as spring takes off, I'll use up my energy and won't have much left for the actualization of my creative work.

PRACTICE: Pick a Project

The game of waiting and sifting is over. You have your lists before you, your maps and your direction. The cup of vibrancy overflows! Now it's time to choose and devote yourself to one or two projects you can complete in the coming seasons. Once you make this decision and commit yourself to the process, you begin to create.

I don't always finish everything in spring, but I definitely get some major drafts in place that I can continue working on throughout the rest of the year. Spring is when you move beyond the outline and into the heart of the work, when you put the flesh on the bones, when you really see the shape of what's to come.

Beyond the overwhelming and exhausting aspects of spring, now we find our equilibrium and drink freely from its steady flow of energy. This can really uplift the feeling of our practice, but how do we harness such intense creativity and thrive in our work? I circle back to plants and my breath for this, but I also assess where I am in other ways that I know affect my process. Try responding to the following prompts in order to see where you can root into the energy of newness and utilize the vibrant quality of spring as a catalyst that will enable you to begin making whatever it is you want to make.

- Write about the areas in your life in which you feel satisfied.

- Describe in detail some of the things you now accept that you once thought were impossible.

- As you envision the next steps for this moment of newness in your practice, write a pep talk for yourself that focuses on an area that feels lacking.

- Name an area of life that feels like it's in alignment. What can you do to maintain, nurture, or celebrate this feeling?

- In what ways is your creative work already tangible? Is there something missing from this that you'd like to add to upcoming projects?

- What do you feel you're able to accomplish this year? Tap into the energy you have right now and imagine how far it can carry you before another season of rest is needed.

- Set a goal for yourself each day—a word count, page count, or time limit—and see how many days you can stick to it. Build your practice around the information you get from what works and doesn't work during these goal-setting periods.

- Set up a schedule for yourself that allows you to carefully use your energy. Spring is a waxing period and your reserve is slowly growing, so how can you dip in freely without draining yourself too quickly?

- Make an inspiration list. What best informs your practice during spring? If you lose focus, read over this list and home in on the energy it supplies.

- Take time to envision the most ideal outcome you can imagine for the projects that are calling to you. Really sit and see yourself in the future space of completion. What does it look like? You don't have to see every detail, just a glimpse will do. Let this vision ground you as you commit to your practice.

Your responses to these prompts should give you an idea of how to balance the scales of your possible projects. Seeing where you are creatively will allow you to more confidently decide on the direction that best suits your current mood. It's not possible to make a mistake and choose the wrong direction. Whichever project asks you to dive in will inform the next steps of your process. Creativity builds off of itself if we let it flow freely.

If you're feeling stuck, practice praise.

Spring is incredibly inspiring with all of its bold beauty and whirling energy. Sometimes it can feel difficult to contain it all within an artwork or practice, so it may feel good to decide on an approach. I often prefer the route of praise and find that I can attempt to accommodate the vast array of spring's fantastic features if I start from a place of admiration.

Lists of gratitude, complimentary poems, and lyrics of rapture seem to be the best fit for honoring this pulsing season. If we set out to revere the psychedelic colors of spring, we set ourselves up for a wonderful experience of exploration, and each artistic effort to praise the beauty of the season aligns us further with its character.

What better way to explore all of this newness than to applaud it? How can you weave this exaltation into your medium? All forms of art are known to highlight the celebratory and congratulatory. It's our job as artists to point out beauty, worship it, and display its power. Spring is such a perfect time of year for this aspect of creative work.

Step outside and look for something that leaves you awestruck. Is it a vernal pond, the bright wing of a bird, the luminous glow of the fresh canopy? Once you find it, focus on praising it with your own poetic interpretation and see how everything that's currently overflowing with the pulse of life is also available as your personal Muse for the season. This is what spring offers us, a booming gift of ceaseless creation that surrounds us with elaborate and inspiring details. In this grand supply, I find encouragement and energy that help me determine the course for my practice.

A Morning

I gladly keep the windows open,
desert air rushing in to cover everything
with chaparral dust. I'll wipe it up again
and again, or just let it stay. The sound
of the cat drinking. The hatchet cut
on my knuckle and the splinters in my hands.
Good to wear the mark of wood.
Old broom handles and the worn barn door.
Avocado, pine and oak. A needle
and the slow yet satisfying meditation
of removal. I praise it all
with water for the orchard roots
and bring the hose to my lips.
I release all worry.
The earth is here and I am it.

PRACTICE: Communication—Get Loud

Each year when spring expresses itself, I'm amazed by how loud it is—every bird call, every color, the excited squirrels, and the booming thunder. It's truly the most flamboyant season, and if I'm committed to the effort of following its lead, I like to let myself get loud too. This is when everything around us moves from unspoken communication to outspoken expression.

I like the way spring encourages me to open up my voice. Try reading poems aloud to the blooming world. Turn the music up and shake your body in honor of all that is busting forth freely. Channel some of that freedom yourself and have a boisterous conversation with the tulips. Go ahead and get loud. Break loose and awaken.

The things that help me get creative aren't always understated or calming. Sometimes I need to sing and dance like a maniac before I can sit down in my chair and write. This moving and singing is an outward expression of the rapport I have with my body, and it helps me get back in touch with my vocal cords after a quiet winter.

I read aloud all the time, but joining the exuberant tone of spring helps me feel more in sync with the season. The way the ground becomes a carpet of color makes me laugh out loud with reckless joy. Play your guitar for the bright new world, put your sculpture in the sun, and howl your delight in its direction. In whatever way feels right, just enjoy however your voice can rise to meet the clamor of the moment.

This is also the time of year when I start craving communication with other people, when I start hanging out, talking things over, and gathering inspiration by way of conversation. This is when I find myself ready to laugh and share meals, plot and plan, joke and be merry with my friends who I probably didn't see too often in the wintertime. Even if I'm slow to emerge, I feel the buzzing desire to dive into discourse as soon as spring becomes obvious.

Notice how the birds speak to one another, their back and forth, their call and response. It's purposeful and calculated and they give each other time to voice whatever it is they need to voice. How do the insects talk? Their buzzing rhythm undulates and builds slowly, expressing a complex language of presence and animation. How can we follow suit when we reconnect in the spring? Here are some questions to ask yourself as the season of communication returns:

- How do you already bring communication into your practice?

- Consider communicating with the landscape around you. What does it look like to connect with the plants, animals, and people in your community? What kind of language exists with each?

- Observe the bursting spring discussions between flora, fauna, and other humans. Try to record one of these conversations and get idealistic with the rapport. See how it inspires you. For example, what do you imagine the robins are talking about? What about the willow trees? The entire world is alive with chatter right now, and it's interesting to imagine how this cacophony affects and adds to our practice.

- Can you find someone new to talk to? Someone locally who sparks your interest? Now is a good time to start seeking out creative confidants and potential collaborators as the season opens us all up to connection.

An Overview of Spring Month by Month

March

I always like to call this the "Month of the Monk" because I never find myself quite ready to leave the satisfying cocoon of winter, and spring is never certain it wants to take hold in March. This is the month with the most vacillation between our deep space of introspection and the outward pull of spring's growth process. In March, we carefully begin finding our way into newness while being very kind to ourselves as we drift back into sleep whenever we can, gradually undulating inward and outward. March is historically a tough month for many people, and I think the warnings are tied directly to the moodiness of this period. Just remember not to ask too much of yourself, to accept the one-step-forward-one-step-back reality, and to let your practice take root in the same way, following the undulating lead of spring.

Celebrating the Spring Equinox

On this day of equal light and dark, we honor the beginning of spring. It's a great time to start letting in the feeling that comes with sunshine and the potency of growth. I welcome spring with an altar, setting my intentions and calling on the guidance of flora and fauna as I show my respect for every living thing that's coming back into view. This is the first moment I really feel the surge of spring as the initial spark of the season thrusts into my awareness. It's during this celebration that I set myself up to shift from slowness into a new speed. The equinox marks the balance point, and from here on out I know my practice will only open up more and more.

April

After the last bouts of isolation in March, April is when we start the second act, the part of spring that keeps the door open a crack so we can remember slowness, but clearly ushers us into the vibrancy of the season that pulses ahead of us. April can be really overwhelming. It's the time of year when everything rises to the surface, when expression and exposure really take hold, and we aren't quite on our feet yet but we're indeed awake. In April, I start to sink myself into my practice. I see what I'll work on, and I begin to own it. I might still have moments that feel exhausting, but the world around me is fully alive in a way that inspires me to join its fervor.

May

By May, I'm in the full swing of spring. The gardens are planted, I find myself outside whenever possible, I wake early to write as much as I can before anyone else is up and mowing their lawn, and I listen to the birds as they unleash their cacophony with the sunrise. Late spring gives hints of summer, so I start reaching out to people, and I find myself remembering what it is that I have to offer the world and what I want to share with others. I also usually have a project or two in full process by this point. Just as the earth bellows with its vitality, I find my body, mind, and spirit are at the height of their creative potential, as long as I've taken good care to rest and restore myself while riding the wave of this dynamic season.

Celebrating May Day or Beltane

There are many cultural traditions surrounding the first of May, as it's often seen as the halfway point between spring and summer. Depending on your background, you might connect with a rich history of earth-based holidays, and this one is commonly known. I like this holiday as a transitional moment in between spring's two phases, and it might help illuminate or solidify your feelings of turning outward if you choose to celebrate it somehow. My favorite way to celebrate this holiday is to dance around a bonfire or spend time in a space that's abundant with flowers, but there are countless ways to usher in the first sensations of summer.

Poems for Spring

"A Purification" – Wendell Berry

"A Cold Spring" – Elizabeth Bishop

"Today" – Billy Collins

"Violets" – Alice Dunbar-Nelson

"Rondeau" – Jessie Redmon Fauset

"Thank You" – Ross Gay

"Primavera" – Louise Glück

"An Earth Song" – Langston Hughes

"Mud Season" – Jane Kenyon

"Spring People" – Audre Lorde

"After the Winter" – Claude McKay

"Spring Dawn" – George Marion McClellan

"Spring" – Edna St. Vincent Millay

"Spring" – W.S. Merwin

"Spring" – Mary Oliver

"The Unfurl" – Mary Ruefle

"It Is A Spring Afternoon" – Anne Sexton

"My Mississippi Spring" – Margaret Walker

"April Morning" – Jonathan Wells

"The Bitter World of Spring" – William Carlos Williams

How to Transition into Summer

Moving from spring to summer is the easiest transition we make because summer is such a welcomed period of togetherness. But be sure not to rush past the power of spring.

As we emerge from the shadows of winter, we come back to one another with stories to share and possibilities to discuss. Even though I sometimes need to prioritize uninterrupted solitude for my creative process, I recognize that other people make up a huge part of my practice, and spring is when I begin to find them again. This is the time of year that I go from seeking a confidant to walking with a friend in a park, and eventually I'll get to the shared expansion of summer, but spring is always the first step in reconnecting.

Just remind yourself of the word *beginning* with everything you do in spring. It's a starting point that wants your voice to awaken, a preamble, an initial launch of what will build into the magic of summertime, a gradual reintroduction. The intention with this season is to slowly ease back into the fold of socialization. In summer I go all out, but for now, I'm mindful of my capacity and caution against getting easily distracted or overwhelmed.

In the summer section, we'll dive deeper into the importance of human connection as it couples with creativity, but for this period of springtime development, think of a few ways you'd like to slowly renew the relationships that may have gone dormant over the winter. Maybe you have some friends you can write letters to or have over for dinner? Maybe you can put on a modest show in your backyard or read a few poems to your neighbors? The point of this blooming season is to begin reviving our ties to the outer world, including to other people. Summer will usher in performance and opportunities for expansive sharing, and spring gives us the chance to progressively and comfortably move into this communal experience.

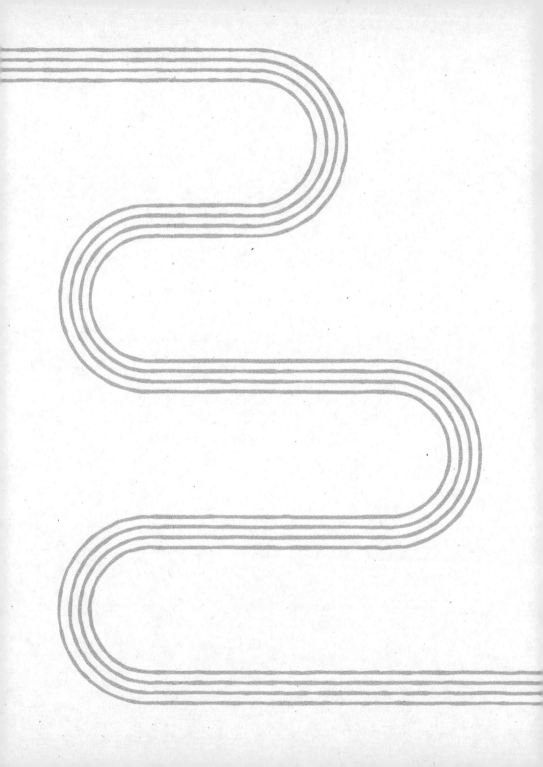

SUMMER

Community – Togetherness – Relaxation
– Openness – Connectivity – Excitement –
Nurturing – Performance – Sharing – Enthusiasm
– Participation – Saturation – Fulfillment
– Validation – Interdependence – Social –
Celebration – Revelry – Collaboration – Ease

***

How do we find ourselves wholly
in the light of the sun?

Together, side by side, sharing
shade and warmth alike.

***

When summer arrives, I'm eager to share my time, space, and work. In this season of sun, I'm excited to get on stage, perform, and commune with my audience, colleagues, and friends. I want to see art, meet with other makers, and witness the collective work we've all been brewing and building in private. I also want to linger in moments of connection, giving myself over to the longer days, letting time pass slowly and in good company.

Summer is when we congregate, delight in the bounty of the garden, eat meals under the shade trees, and partake in discussions about our progress and setbacks. This is the season of togetherness.

Creative practice can be very personal and internal, but for most artists, it feels important to share our work, even if with just a sacred few. I've carefully explored some of my favorite ways to show up in the world of relationships when it comes to my practice. I find that sunshine and good weather help us all come fully out into the open, and when we do, we're more relaxed, ready and willing to receive inspiration or share our offerings with enthusiasm.

Summer is a celebratory time, when we've gotten used to the exposure of spring and feel a sense of confidence when it comes to bringing our creations out into the light. It's a grounded time of surplus that doesn't ask us to rush. Summer makes me feel looser, much more at ease, and more available to my community. I get into discussions with my neighbors, I dawdle outside as long as possible to enjoy the warm nights, and I consider how to showcase everything I've been working on in the previous months. This season of heat and leisure also makes room for my desire to travel, host people, explore the outer world, and express myself creatively at the same time. I'm no longer cautious with my outward energy or inclined to hermit away, but wholly excited to exhibit my findings.

Togetherness

When the river says *swim*, we swim.

The plants all lean low in the midday
heat, full of sun's brilliant wisdom.

Everyone gathers at the banks, dipping in
the cool water, in the calm shade.

Listen to the steady song of the bullfrog.
Watch the careful fish as they get larger.

Butterflies dot the open skies and dragonflies
deliver their dancing messages.

This is the outcome revealed, ours to
revel in after seasons of growth.

See how all presents itself in maximum form?

This bold collection of detailed
results is meant to be shared.

May we bow and sing along accordingly, showing
each other what resides in our hearts.

Air balmy around us, we congregate and find relief.

Here is a seat on the blanket and
ample space for reclining.

Now is our opportunity to celebrate,
to exalt our endless story,

to relax into the beauty of it all side by side.

Prompts from the Planet

What do plants and other animals do in the summer?

They fill themselves up with the bounty that surrounds them.

They buzz and open wider. Foxes gorging on berries, bears catching fish together, elk surveying the lush meadows in unison. Everyone is alight and alive in their fullest form, activated, on the move, exploring and eating well.

See how the snake sleeps peacefully in the sun. See how the flowers execute their wildest colors.

All partake in the light, lounging limp in the afternoon, not too hasty, and yet wholly available.

Remember, we are part of the same cycle.

Remember to ask yourself: *What is the natural world up to right now? How does it include me? How is it my mirror?*

PRACTICE: Creative Community, Connection & Collaboration

Summer is the perfect time of year to bring other people into your practice. Sometimes, after the rush of spring, I need to slow down and consider the best ways to reach out, what plans suit my current projects, and who makes the most sense to collaborate with. Gathering together is best when the energy is relaxed and excited all at once, but that kind of magic takes deliberation to conjure up effectively.

Here are some questions and prompts to get you thinking about your connection to your creative community as you begin to make summer plans with others.

- In what ways do/don't you feel part of community?

- Where do you feel you most belong?

- What are some acts of service that you regularly perform?

- Write a list of people you would like to thank and the reasons for your gratitude.

- What is one thing you enjoy that others often don't?

- What is one thing you dislike that others often like?

- Write a list of your current boundaries, the healthy limitations you uphold in your life to support yourself and others.

- Name some of the teachers that are currently in your life and write about what they teach you.

- Now, consider if there are new things you'd like to learn and seek out teachers who might support your expansion.

- What are your thoughts on friendship? In your opinion, what's the difference between a friend and an acquaintance?

- What does the word *loyalty* bring up for you?

- How do you feel about the concept of commitment?

- Is there a group you can join that can enrich your creative practice in a new and interesting way?

Although summer is a very extroverted time of year, it's important to recognize which people fill you up and support your practice best. Setting aside time to meditate on this before stepping into the whirlwind of socializing will put you on a more balanced path and help prevent overwhelm. Just because the sun is out and the parties are rolling doesn't mean you're suited for it all. I value using my intuition as I form a healthy vision of my most fulfilling summer interactions.

At this point in my life, I have people in various places who I want to visit regularly, and I like to build my plans around them. Who haven't I seen in a while? Who has been asking to be a part of my latest project? Can you list some spaces you'd like your artwork to inhabit?

Because summer is about output, that means everyone around us is stepping toward some outward practice as well, whether it's big or small. Everyone has something to share, whether it's the bounty from their garden, a conversation about their past months of artistic process, or a fun puppet show hosted in their backyard. This is the season that reminds us of how much energy and motivation we offer one another.

There are many aspects of my creative work that I cannot do alone. The communal charge of summer gets me excited about the possibilities of collaboration. So much of my process happens in solitude, but when I return to community, I find a certain spark that's crucial for my artistic growth. I know I don't contain every skill needed to bring all of my ideas into completion. My friends help me carry out all of my dreams, artistic or otherwise, and this is the season that encourages me to flock to them for insight, aid, and amplification. Spending time with other artists always enriches my thoughts around my practice and inspires conceptual development. In togetherness, we blend with one another, our mediums expand, and we discover unique outlets for expression that wouldn't exist otherwise.

Try writing a list of ten people you want to connect with this summer and flesh out the creative ties you have with them. How can you possibly collaborate? What can they offer your creative practice? How do they uplift your voice? Is there a new craft you feel could harmonize with your current one? Maybe someone in your community can help make this happen. By the time the weather gets hot, we're no longer spending our days alone diving into our depths. In the bright sunshine, we're able to see ourselves through our experiences with others, and this can offer unique and impactful revelations.

Collaboration is always an experiment, so as you bring your personal practice to the table, try to stay open and let the process flow between you and your collaborator without a rigid idea of an outcome. Sometimes the best collaborations come from simply being with other people and witnessing whatever reverberation occurs between you. So much of my inspiration comes from moments of connection that enable me to further know myself. To see my behavior and experience my feelings in relationship with others is an expansive gift that directly affects my artistic self. The people who come into my world add to my story, they bring out aspects of my personality that I cannot discover on my own, and they often give me the intricate context in which a poem reveals itself.

As summer is a sensual season, our focus on relationships often rises into the realm of romance this time of year. The line between creative and sexual energy is very thin. These energies naturally feed off of one another, and that's why we often become each other's Muses. Think of how many masterpieces are brought into fruition this way. Summer romance can be an incredible source of inspiration, causing us to create poems, songs, paintings, or other expressions in the name of love.

I never undervalue the effect shared passion has on my practice. The introspective portals that open up when we're committed to diving into the depths of one another are limitless. This kind of bond has influenced some of the greatest artists throughout time, and summer is such a perfect season to explore the many ways affection and desire expand our ability to creatively respond to the world around us.

May the sensuality of the season activate and propel you to tap into the epic reserves of inspiration that love likes to unfurl. Ask yourself how your sensuality links to your practice. Is it a source of fire and enthusiasm in your life? By no means do you have to be in partnership to experience the thrill and spark of romance. But try to tap into this wellspring in a steamy and exciting way. It's worth examining how this carnal energy directly heightens our creative output, and as the relationships develop, so do the lessons and insights.

Devil's Elbow

Rushing river that hooks
around black rock and cuts
its course with a sharp bend.
I was brought here
by three different lovers.
Once to burn branches on the shore.
Once to remove our clothes
and swim all the way across.
Once to jump from the highest rock
so that I would follow.

The fire wouldn't start.
The other side was swamp.
The rock was not that high.
The devil is in the memories,
a shadow of disappointment,
but light lives on in the water.

I went back the following summer
with three women. We were well received
by the calm current and the sun
stretching its rays below the surface.
We napped naked on the shore, soaked
our brown skin and spoke
to the swimming snake.
We sang our spells, opened
apricots for the bees and saw
a white dog on the hillside.
I had never stayed so long
without growing cold.
Could it be that a place
with such a title only
wants a witch?

The Work That Cannot Be Done Alone

I'm so much happier
when I'm by myself. I can go
at least seven days without seeing
another human. I'm the hermit
in the desert, but I eventually ache
to show the sunrise to someone.
The work of love proves
that I'm more than a gritty animal.
I see the hole in my heart
fill with ash when you arrive,
a sign that I need to be held.
My brain cannot grow
without your eyes staring into mine.
I cannot be good without knowing
how to surrender, how to let you
be both a child and a man in my arms.
Relationships are a cosmic handout.
A challenge sits between me and my lover—
an infinity mirror that I can withstand
only because this person knows
when to cover my face.
Togetherness reveals a realm
as deep and hot as a volcano.
We'll burn up in there
if we do it right.

PRACTICE: Creative Conversation

One of the best ways to gather inspiration is to engage in stimulating conversation, and summertime offers many opportunities for this. Anything that helps me know myself in a deeper way is beneficial for my writing practice, and talking with inquisitive people provides an incredible avenue for self-exploration.

Throughout the warmer months there are countless ways to conjure up creative conversations. Everyone is out and about, and there are always parties, art shows, events in the park, picnics, and concerts. But my favorite recipe for getting into a good talk is to plan a small summer dinner party with no more than ten people who I think will align in some way. It's an art all its own to bring together the right blend of people, so if this idea intrigues you, really think hard about how each person will elevate the overall experience.

After you figure out the meticulous list of curious and open-minded guests, serve up a simple summer feast and see what happens. In these comforting and exciting moments, I like to test out my new ideas, explore my insights, and indulge in the mirror that other people provide for my practice. These are the moments that tend to motivate me. It's so fun to hear about other people's creative concepts, feel out where we connect, receive their energy, and appreciate the innovative surprises that surface as we share our opinions and desires. It's best when it's a reciprocal exchange of interest and query. The treasures I collect during these conversations touch my work for months, sometimes even years to come.

Ideas to Inspire Dinner Party Conversation

- Ask everyone to bring a short poem to share. My friends in L.A. host pasta and poetry nights that always spur really heartfelt and profound discussion.

- Ask guests to share what they're currently working on in a salon-style format that allows each person to talk while everyone else listens. This is a great way to receive one another without the need for comment or critique. I often do this with my friends, and not always at the dinner table.

- Make it a themed dinner to expand inspiration. Maybe you could ask each person to make a seasonal dish or you can re-create a surrealist dinner party. Themes help give guests a direct and creative point of reference, which acts as a bridge for connection. I love themed parties because it's so interesting to see how each person approaches the motif in their own special way.

- Ask everyone to bring an item for a group altar dedicated to creativity and expression or something else that's central to the moment in time you're all sharing. A summer altar is always a good choice, as it showcases gifts from the garden and usually overflows with flowers and fruits. Additionally, group altars are a great way to bring folks into an intentional yet playful act. There's a spiritual quality of purpose and prayer built into making the altar, and it inevitably grows into a charged space of beauty and collaboration.

- Get everyone to write their desired conversation topics on pieces of paper, then randomly pull each one from a hat. Normally it won't be difficult to find things to talk about in these settings, but it can be really energizing to shift the energy at the table and help everyone connect over a shared focus. Pulling from a hat brings in a sense of levity and a game-like quality, so even if the topics get heavy, you can always pass the hat and switch up the mood.

- Ask each person to talk about their summer plans. I like moving from person to person and engaging in focused group listening, but some people don't like to be put on the spot. Asking folks to talk about their summer plans is an easy outlet for casual conversation that allows people to catch up and gives them an opportunity to relate.

- Get everyone to go outside at some point in the evening. This change in setting always helps progress imaginative conversation because the energy shifts, people break off into their own private moments of connection, and everyone gets to enjoy the fresh air.

- Invite each person to give an overview of their personal practice. If you want to get right into the heart of artistic conversation, ask everyone to discuss their current process. How folks approach their creativity in summer is always interesting, and it's a good reference point that can help some people get on track and aid others in loosening up. This can be salon style as well, or it can just be something to ask in other casual moments of conversation.

Throughout generations, people have talked around the dinner table. The casual openness of summer really supports this method of deciphering our inner workings with others. Don't underestimate the importance of deep discussion when it comes to artistic process. Usually, you won't need to do much to inspire this kind of conversation if you invite a dynamic group of guests. I find that this type of safe space for sharing and reflection is crucial for most people.

Creative conversation is the buzzing result of summer shared; it's that burning link that lives between us, and it's an opportunity to hand the fire back and forth freely. I know I'm more of an introvert than an extrovert, garnering my energy when I'm alone in my process, but I also understand the worth of outside insight and how impactful it is to receive this motivation.

If you're feeling stuck or overwhelmed, return to the practice of listening and presence.

Summer vibrates with vigorous instruction. Everything is in its highest state—the flowers full of bees, the branches humming with cicadas. When the nonstop fun of the season wears on me, I like to take a walk and return to the practice of listening. Every aspect of the natural world is steady in its summer output. Fruits ripen; insects multiply; birds and bats fly low, eating freely in the warm evening; and trees express their greenest leaves.

Yet, unlike the fervor of spring, the hottest months are bustling but held by a sense of stasis. When I hear the world in this condition of fullness, established in its seasonal equilibrium, I feel at ease, as if everything is just as it should be, as if the work of the planet has once again come to fruition and I'm part of it.

Together, we have all arrived, made it through another bout of cold and growth, here to find the nourishment of the sun, to hear the wild song of everything in its health and fullness. With this listening meditation, I return to a feeling of looseness and this is where my summer creativity dwells. When I land in this space of resonance, surrounded by the pulse of heat, I breathe a bit deeper and often find a poetic notion waiting for me within the hum.

My God Comes to Me

As the light swimming up
the thick arc of the oak tree.
I am transfixed by this spell of sun
that keeps my eyes rhythmically rolling
up and down the big gnarled body, observing
lit moss and waxy poison oak vines.
The golden beams are a surreal wave
and I am mesmerized, blissful, deeply calm.

Until a branch falls on the tin roof
like a gong for splitting silence, a bell
of mindfulness without an echo.
I note my heartbeat for the first time in a while
and watch my shirt collar rise and fall
with a quick throbbing pulse.

I consider this a divine interruption
reminding me to breathe deeper. I turn back
to watch the wind make silver dollars out of leaves.
I gaze at a glow that mimics water
even if there isn't a stream nearby,
a rippled reflection as the branches
sway, and again I find my elemental trance.

PRACTICE: Knowing Your Audience

At this point in the year, you most likely have a portion of creative work that feels ready to share. Maybe winter allowed you the time to finish a project, and it's ready to be fully revealed. Maybe you're only halfway through or you have a rough draft that you need someone else's eyes on. Whatever the state of your work, this is the season to invite someone else into your process.

Who is your ideal audience? As we bring our ideas into fruition, different points on the timeline of creation call for different audiences. If you need helpful critique, you may seek the careful eye of an editor or a workshop group that will comment on your writing. If you feel like you're finished with something, set up an event to showcase it. Play your new song at a dinner party, invite someone over and read them an excerpt of your novel in the garden, or show someone images of your newest paintings as you hang out at the beach. It doesn't have to be a grand effort, just an opening up of your process, an invitation for others to experience what you make.

Sharing our work invites a sense of validation and affirmation. Bringing an audience into our creative practice is like saying, "This thing I made is truly worth something to me," and it suggests that whatever your creative spirit inspires isn't just a selfish act of pleasure but a request for others to join in the exploration.

You can keep it really small and still fulfill the importance of sharing. Who can you call on when you're in need?

Why do you trust them? Can you make time to share your creative expression with them? We don't always have to make a big fuss out of performing our artwork. Sharing can be extremely low-key and intimate yet still so satisfying.

As you move into the sharing nature of summer, get clear on what you'd like to share and who you want to share it with. How does your artwork ask to be demonstrated? How can you articulate the inner world that brings you so much joy and energy? Imagine what you can learn about your artwork through the way others witness and receive it. The interdependence that summer highlights can easily spread into our creative practice, and this opportunity for reflection will expand our understanding of how something so personal can indeed affect and enliven others.

Keep in mind that you may not feel the need to share your work with other people at all. This is worth examining. Sometimes I write things and never read them to other humans, but I'll share them with the trees, the wildflowers, the mountains, the valley, or the ocean. It can be just as satisfying for me to recite my poems to the sky as it is for me to share them with an audience of people in a bookstore. It depends on the work, and it depends on my mood. Your vision for sharing will evolve over time if you lean in and decipher what works best for you as you grow in your practice. Summer gives us the relaxed space to feel out our desires around artistic congregation and exposure.

I Live in the Woods

I have a splinter in my palm
from the Beltane bonfire.
I wish I had a horse to ride
into town. Last night I finished
reading *Pilgrim at Tinker Creek*—
I read the whole book aloud to no one.

The big paper wasp nest fell on the trail
and I don't need to touch this one
to know how it'd feel in my hands.

Some creature vomited grass
right at the base of my doorstep
and there is a white moth stretched open
flat and wide on a sword fern.
There goes the slick black cat and the small
brown cricket—both cross over
the bear prints on the porch.

I harvested the burdock—dug down
50 inches into thick dark soil to find
the end of the root and pulled it up whole.

At dusk I trimmed the new buds
of doug fir to mix with fresh
ginger and boiling water for tea.
I spoke to the valley and it didn't
answer in English, but it did answer.
Two trees are rubbing together—I can
hear them singing in high-pitched notes.
They are stuck side by side in growth,
holding one another up, defining this night.

PRACTICE: Planning Your Performance

Summer is a great time to perform your work in public. Making this happen will take a lot of energy and every element of your planning skills, but it doesn't need to be stressful. When I plan a performance schedule, I think about the friends I want to share my work with and where they are in the world. How can I bring my creative gifts to them? What's the best way to share what I've been crafting?

I'm a big fan of DIY tours, and I've been organizing them for myself since I was nineteen. I drive around the country and spend time singing; dancing; reading poems in basements, living rooms, and bookstores; and hardly making any money but fully enjoying the experience of communion. When an artist comes to town, they often have something to offer, and I've always found this to be the most fulfilling way to travel. If you show up with your heart on your sleeve and your inner world in your outstretched hands, the entire town may welcome you with intrigue and gratitude.

In order to plan your performance trip, just think of who you want to visit and how you can put on a show in their town. Think of someone you frequently miss. Can you visit them and share your work, even if it's just the two of you? Performance planning requires a lot of reflection about your relationships. Consider doing even more work around your sense of community and connections as you begin to bring your performance ideas into fruition.

It doesn't matter what your medium is, it's always possible to find large and small ways to showcase your creations. Your friends and supporters will honor your effort by showing up and engaging. In the winter, I make a list of places and people I'd like to visit, and then when summer comes along I've already put the plan in motion by reaching out ahead of time. But it can be last minute too. Performance success is fully based on a balance of your planning abilities and chance, so as long as your expectations are reasonable, you'll be doing what really matters: sharing your work.

Sometimes my shows are really small, like a living room full of friends, but with such an intimate audience, I can usually see who is moved and why. Hang your paintings in someone's garage-turned-gallery, put on your play in small-town parks, or rent out a local community center and sing your heart out. I once hosted a poetry reading on a sailboat. If you allow yourself to bring your work into the world with a sense of amusement and exploration, your audience will bring their curiosity and openness in exchange.

A stage can appear anywhere. I once led a group of twenty or so people down one of my favorite trails, ending up in a spruce grove where I read them a collection of my new poems. Take some time to envision and write down at least five scenarios of inventive, inspirational performances. Make sure each ideal experience includes who, what, where, and when. Afterward, you can build a trip, tour, or even just a few local visits around this list.

Offering your artwork to your friends, family, and supporters is a direct way of showing them your gratitude. Anyone who cares about you wants to know what you've been brewing in your studio. It definitely takes some confidence and bravery to expose your creative practice in this way, but performance is not just about you; it's about community, exchange, and engagement. The easeful energy of summer will support you in this experiment of presenting your imaginative achievements.

If you're feeling stuck, remember to have fun.

Summer's foundation holds the mood of vacation. Whatever plans you make, let the feeling of fun and relaxation lead you. If I ever get overwhelmed by the full plate of summer, I remind myself to be playful with it first and foremost. Let the weight of your responsibilities melt in the sun a bit; lean into the listlessness and try to focus on your deepest delight.

Summer is a hedonistic time. It's a time of release and pleasure, so if you find yourself with a deadline or something pressing to get accomplished in these months, see if you can turn toward the joy of it. Can you take your work outside? Can you set up an umbrella in the shade and do your business? Can you pause and have a very brief dance party when things feel too serious? Can you set aside an hour or two in the afternoon to go for a swim somewhere?

Try your best to loosen up in these months of sun and revelry. Don't be too hard on yourself because summer is openly our shared excuse for slowness, lethargy, and celebration. At some point, it can be painful to ignore the sheer glee it provides, so I always do my best to lead with light-heartedness in this season that asks us to explore, expand, and enjoy ourselves.

Fortify

Put your body in the sunshine.

Feel the ease of warm muscles moving.

What midday sleep provides is a dream like no other,

warm reverie that sticks in the mind and gives renewal.

This is when the spirit speaks as if it were honey.

It pours over everything with sweet sensuality.

There is no quick stop, no harsh freeze or deep demand.

As the thunderstorm delivers its wisdom in wind,

we are struck with clarity like lightning,

and yet we feel no need to jump up in quick expression.

Everything comes out easy now, unhurried

and cupped by cricket song.

Summer isn't typically a very productive time for me. I'm so excited to reunite with my community that I don't plan on completing projects or focusing inward too often. This is my time to surface, to surrender to the languid nature of the season, and let it take me where it must, usually to some body of water.

But I don't abandon my artistry just because I'm busy sweating and socializing. It takes some careful forethought to make sure I keep up with my work when the sun is booming outside and all my friends want to hang out. In summer, just as I do every other season, I ask myself what I'm capable of and what I'm actually able to accomplish with the amount of time and energy I have. I get over-whelmed if I don't consistently check in with my capacity. Summer offers the perfect balance of winding down in the slow seduction of heat and rallying to make some fun, communal events happen.

If creativity rises up in the summer, it's usually much more spontaneous than in the other months. It's in this hot season that I really allow myself to get distracted, make things whenever I feel like it, and release the rhythm of my discipline. Summertime is meant for laziness, spon-taneous trips to the beach, and sudden bursts of creative output followed by backyard barbeques.

In other seasons, I'm more inclined to fall into a dedi-cated pattern of work, but in summer, I let myself get loose and enjoy a more impromptu practice. This experience affects my work all year long, as I often call on the freedom of summer when I get too bogged down or stringent with myself in later months. Every season gives us an opportunity to look at the balance of rest and diligence that upholds our imaginative effort.

In the midst of all this outward expression, I find that, above all else, summer is a really nurturing time, a period that allows us to relax together and explore and connect in an untethered state. It can be a heightened experience of events and travel, but within these adventures is the understanding that if there's a swimming hole on the way, there's definitely time to stop. Along with the power of connection and performance, summer provides us with an exhale, a space to unwind, and in this space, we're free to share our discoveries without pressure.

ELEMENTAL INSTRUCTION: Fire

Fire is the element assigned to the first half of summer. Everything is alight with sun. Passion and pleasure take the forefront. Burning desire aligns with these hot months. A sense of renewal and healing warmth ushers our bodies, minds, and spirits into relaxation. It's a bright time of sensuality and heightened emotion that brings us together in eagerness and excitement.

But remember that fire also holds grief and death. With summer wildfires, we're reminded that everything is made to burn brilliantly toward its end. There can be a sadness in summer, a longing for what was, a flicker of understanding that although we're in our outward flash of shared spirit, we aren't made for constant sun. The mood is often described as choleric. We can get irritable in the heat, tired and worn, oversaturated and scorched.

Notice how you react to summer's fiery character. Do you carry a flame of inspiration, charged and ready to consume input, and expend yourself freely? Can you bring balance to your burning? In what ways do you enjoy feeding the blaze of the season, and in what ways do you notice yourself getting singed? Can you harness the fever of summer and combine it with your creative efforts?

Nothing Will End

We drive up the Pacific Coast Highway
to the place where the big black rocks
make a pyramid. You remember it
from your one solo trip years ago.
You're hardly ever alone now.

Skipping up to the edge, I can tell
you think that this will always be here.
I want to say *this will all fall into the ocean soon.*

We walk the trail in Malibu
where the oaks are old and black,
marked with the cribbage of birds.
The poison oak reaches, red and dusty.
This will all burn in wildfire soon.

We round the corner and somehow,
in all of this heat, in the scorch of summer,
the pond is full and blooming green with bull rush,
a lacework of algae decorating the surface.
We've never seen it wet before,
usually we trace the chips of clay
and look for animal prints.

I attribute this miracle to your
naiveté, your willingness to believe
that nothing will end, that everything
will keep on with its beauty.
And you're right.
This place will change.
Great suffering will occur.
The Pacific will swallow
so much, but the earth
it will survive us.

The second half of summer calls on the element of earth. As we move into autumn, we're fully supported by the planet, nurtured and held as our energy begins its reliable turn inward. We're surrounded by abundance as the harvest rises to its peak and we're nourished by the spectacular yield that earth offers up every year.

Late summer asks us to sing songs of praise in unison as the fields provide us with everything we need. In this time, we feel the burn begin to lessen as the fire retreats, and we lean deeper into the healing presence of the ground.

How can you align with this shift and connect with the earth as summer wanes? As you begin to receive the great endowment of the harvest, this shift will carry you into fall. This is an important moment that is wholly facilitated by the land. How will you accept this honor? What kind of ritual will mark this time for you? Can you plant your feet on the ground and accept its guidance? Let your place on the planet supply you with its support, and the adjustment that autumn bestows will be easier to accept.

PRACTICE: Stealing Time for Practice

Summer is full. The garden is bursting with bounty and the days are long, packed with people and adventure, so if I ever find a moment of inspiration in the midst of it all, I do my best to use it. Unlike any other season, summer makes my practice really random, less scheduled and reliable. Knowing this, I try to steal moments for writing whenever I can.

For example, as I'm writing this it's late August. Summer is waning, and I'm squeezing in every possible boating and swimming adventure. I'm socializing as much as I can before the days get shorter. But yesterday there was a glorious thunderstorm, and the power went out. My phone wasn't working, the internet was out, and the river was full of dirty rainwater. It was the perfect excuse to sit down and write!

I always attempt to put my writing practice ahead of everything else, but in summer the priority lessens a bit and I appreciate this change that takes me out into the world more. Still, I always try to seize the best moments for creation, and it takes particular awareness to utilize these stray windows of summer focus. It may be hard to get up early if you've been on the dance floor all night, but if you wake up before dawn with an urge to carve out a moment in your studio, do it! Then maybe you can take a midafternoon nap when the heat of the day makes creativity feel impossible.

A lot of my friends have to work all summer long because the weather is so nice. This is their seasonal crunch time for money-making because they are builders and farmers. Waking up with the sun and working late into the evening in the fields or on rooftops, they too have to find a way to steal moments of practice within the long-lit days. Summer is when morning folks sometimes turn into night owls; we often shift according to the sun and our waves of stamina, finding different ways to sneak in bouts of practice. I like this process of figuring, bending and moving with the season. Our busiest times can provide us with an appreciation and keen eye for appearances of the summer Muse who breezily instructs us to sit down and make something whenever we can.

The power is sure to come back on soon, but until then I'll treasure my secret time and space, which allows me to tap into a winter-like hermit mood, writing without interruption and preparing for the inward shift of fall.

If you're feeling stuck, align with the sun.

Above all else, the sun is the master of summer. If you feel adrift, lazy, or disconnected, return to the sun as your guide. What does this burning ball of fire inspire in you? What action (or inaction) does its relentless gaze suggest? Find shade! Take a nap! Get in the cold bathtub and pause! Summer is a charged season of ongoing festivities, but it's also a time to take it easy and soften.

If you lose track of this balance, turn to the sun for direction. It might be that you need to pull out the lounge chair and put the sprinklers on while you eat watermelon popsicles. It might be time to get in a hammock and read that lighthearted novel you've kept on your nightstand for months. Our bodies are nurtured by the summer light and slower pace so we can enter the darker months ahead renewed and refreshed.

My schedule in the summer revolves around the sun. I'm sensitive to the heat, and I make sure to utilize the coolest parts of the day as I build my creative pace. I can't ask myself to write anything cohesive when my brain is in a heat haze. On a really hot day, I can either hole up in the AC and get some writing done, or I can turn outward and go to the lake with my friends. I'm fine with abandoning my practice if I know I'm too burnt out to get any satisfying work done. Sometimes the sun on my skin charges me up and gives me tons of energy, and other days it's too much and I need to retreat indoors. It's a mixture of my mood and the sun's mood, and I accept the process of feeling out this blend all summer long.

I Call the Sun Umalet

I have chased The Sun
my entire life. From childhood
in Florida, through the Andes,
into Athens. Always summer,
always bright, my path of light.

Now I feel the need to honor our fat star
with a unique and holy title.

I climb the long hill to find flat land
beside the tiny orchard. A few sapling trees,
some branches bowing with apples' weight—
pink flesh, yellow skin, cores
kept for next year's crop.
Trunks torn orange where the bears
like to do their damaging dance—where
I myself decide to dance in praise
of The Sun's new name. Naked
and barefoot, flailing for an hour,
going golden and singing
the gibberish language of searching.

Mumbling meditation, howling
and rejoicing in the magic of such illumination,
finally one word starts its significant repetition:
Umaletaaaaa, Umaletaaa,
UMALET.
The name sticks.

Each day I thank Umalet for rising, for setting,
and for returning again. I remain faithful
even in a scorching heat, the drought
that whips us with its harsh hand,
the desert beam that bakes our land.

Still we orbit its glow, its radiance
gives shape to seed, its fire worthy
of our reverence, our divine
and personal designation.

PRACTICE: Shedding

In summer we shed our layers of clothing, and other animals shed their hair, fur, and skin. Come fall, many plants join this process of casting off as well. I notice that as I discard my attire, I feel lighter and exposed in other ways too. This unburdened feeling is a cornerstone of summertime. What can we leave behind as we move freely during this season of ease? What can we let go of in our practice that doesn't fit during these months of sunshine and levity? Are you putting too much pressure on yourself to accomplish and complete things when you should really be putting your to-do list down and joining your friends for a canoeing adventure?

Spring gives us space to clean and organize, allowing us to purge our belongings and arrange our surroundings, but summer suggests a different kind of freedom. Its spirit is nimble, lively, and lightweight, and I adjust my behavior accordingly. Like the dog or the horse, I leave my thick coat behind, and I feel inspired to reveal more, to be more vulnerable. Like the cicada, I become exposed and steady myself for flight, for a transformation that moves me from one phase to the next with a calm deftness.

Carefully observe what you're shedding this summer. What worries or constrictions can you wash away in the water? How can you adjust your discipline so it thaws out a bit and adapts with the weather? What can you put down in order to better fill your arms with the ripe fruits and vegetables that are in season? How can you adapt in order to let this be a period of peace and enjoyment? What can you let go of so you can gain what the sun wants to give you?

PRACTICE: Summer Cleanse

The art of connecting my mind with my body becomes a bit more simplified in summertime. My muscles are loose and warm, I'm much more active, and my understanding around what my body needs is more direct. I need ice water. I need cold grapefruit. I need a nap because it's over ninety degrees. I can stretch so much easier because my spine is already relaxed after swimming in the river. I'm also not sitting at my desk as much, so I'm less constricted in that way as well.

In this freedom, I'm more inclined to do a cleanse. A winter cleanse with broth and whole foods is great, but in the winter, I'm hungry for comforting meals, and I don't want fruit or juice. In the heat of summer, a cucumber or a glass of carrot juice is fulfilling. Fresh food is plentiful and more available, so eating becomes more straightforward and cleaner without much added effort. I'm not a cleansing expert, but I've followed some healthy guidelines and practices over the years based on what foods are in season during summer.

Finding a cleanse that's right for you is important when it comes to creative practice. Sometimes my cleanse only has to take place over a few days and I feel lighter, cleared of the previous season's weight, and ready to relax and reset.

There are benefits to a ritual that feels aligned with heat, sweat, and centering for the next phase of work to come. There's plenty of guidance out there about a variety of respected and traditional cleanses, and I recognize that centering this practice around food isn't for everyone, but in my experience, letting myself shift my connection to food and revive it after a few days of juice or fasting really helps me redefine my personal rhythm, and this directly shows up in my writing.

Humans have been cleansing their bodies with a change in diet during the heavy heat of summer for a very long time. If you haven't considered this before, I recommend seeking someone to guide you toward a cleansing process that's right for you. There are many folks who can hold space for us while we do the work of clearing ourselves. When done in a safe and thoughtful way, a proper cleanse can provide a spiritual experience, heighten your senses, and directly influence your creative mindset.

Staying with Angela

Underneath the rustling eucalyptus,
I spot the dead mourning dove on its back.
Its downy breast moves in the breeze
and looks like breath, but it's not.
The bird tells a story about the cat.
The chimes sing their daily song in my stillness
and the sun arrives with a gentle heat.
When I walk through the front door
I see a rattlesnake coiled below
the climbing rose, resting on the cold
wet sand. Angela brews cacao and cuts
an orange with hands that mother every gift
grown from earth. Her desert willow
blooms pink and white trumpets
for the bees. I sit in its small, tangled
cave of branches to drink fruit juices, to let
my body rest with words like mango and melon.
We practice here among all other
practicing plants and creatures,
growing in the silence, finding our
rhythm with the moon, making prayer
out of every detail collected in the basin.
When we spill honey, the ants come to eat it.

PRACTICE: Swimming

Water and creativity are connected in many ways. The flow of creative practice has its own tides, waves, and varied depths. Water serves as one of my meditation tools throughout the year when it comes to connecting to my creative spirit. I like the mantra, "Let creativity be like water." Repeating this allows my imagination to loosen, shift with its own rhythm, and wash over me.

I'm a big fan of swimming whenever possible, no matter the season, but summer calls me to submerge more often, escaping the heat, cleansing and cooling myself. Even if you aren't a swimmer, I suggest going to a body of water during summer. Find a lake, a pond, a river, the ocean, or even a pool will do. If you aren't drawn to be in the water, simply being near it will give some of the same purification that comes from dunking in or moving through it. And drinking it is obviously crucial, even more so in summertime. Make yourself big jars of water with flower essences, minerals, honey, salt, cucumber, and whatever else it takes to keep you hydrated and connected to this key element as the sun propels energy in and out of you.

When I lived in Los Angeles, getting to the ocean wasn't always easy, and on the hot summer days that I couldn't make the drive, I'd fill my bathtub with cold water and get in and out of it all day long like it was my personal spring. I moved from the tub to my writing desk to the bed for a nap and back again into the tub. If my mind got foggy while I was trying to work, I'd dunk my head in the bath and emerge with a fresh point of view. Don't worry, I was very aware of the drought. When I was finished, I'd always reuse the water for my houseplants.

I also keep a spray mister filled with rosewater on hand at all times. I put it in the fridge during summer and spray my face throughout the day, especially if I'm trying to get in some productive hours of writing. Cold water gives me a reset. It brings me back to myself, especially when the temperature is scorching and my brain feels scrambled.

Connecting with the gift of water during summer is a reliable ritual. I go under the surface and I return to breathe anew. I feel stilted by the humid air, then I drench myself in coldness, electric with a different attitude. If you need a summer refresh, take yourself for a swim.

Midwives of Newborn Symbology

As we jump the cement ledges
of the salmon hatchery
to feed begging mouths briny pellets,
I memorize the way you hesitate.

Our fingers are stained by blackberries, our lips
are mantled with summer, and
we keep silent to hear
the pink bellies rolling over one
another in the humming current.

We walk down the riverbed that is
mostly dry like the deer spine
I found resting in the fernbrake, and I gather stones
for your mother: green granite and forgotten iron.

Damp clay and a smell of must
guide us toward a deep
pool, where we undress, swim
exposed to ancient redwoods,
stomachs tight with chill, hair laced with sand.

As we crouch over the shoreline, our skin dries
by the tongue of the sun and we carve
our crooked symbols into silt.

PRACTICE: Fullness

As I turn to the plants in summertime, I'm struck by their growth, the way they push past any type of tame measurement when soaked in sun. The zucchinis, cucumbers, beans, and tomatoes burst beyond the borders of their boxes. The flowers multiply with endless purpose. The crown of every tree gets larger, and the grass requires tending again so soon after it's mowed. What are these botanical teachers saying to us with their overgrown ritual? What reaching lesson is making itself obvious in every blossom, branch, berry, and leaf? I'm always eager to follow their wise lead. In summer, it seems they're telling us to fill up, rejoice, push past our limits, and reach higher.

I take their advice to heart and apply their relentless propagation to my practice. Summer gives us so much bounty, but not just from the garden's yield. This time of year provides us with plentiful experience, an overflowing cup of escapades and events. Everything that washes over me in summer charges my battery and offers me a surge of subject matter to pull from in the coming months of introspection. Part of my job as an artist in summertime is to drink freely from the wonder of the world, to abandon myself in the gifts of growth without too much thought on how I'll weave it all together later. At this point, we've all achieved our yearly bloom and now is the time to relish it.

The plant world says to stretch further, get sweeter and bigger and better. Collect the nutrients of the earth and openly adore this part of the process. How else will you live well throughout the rest of the year? Summer is your time for all-inclusive replenishment. This is when your notebooks fill with one-liners and quips that will later turn into full-blown stories and compositions. You can begin creating something incredible right now, but if the sky starts speaking in thunderous pink clouds, you will rise from your desk and stand on the porch in awe, collecting the moment like a meal, letting the summer fill you in excess, beyond the brim, confirming that you have everything you need and reminding you that the earth is such a glorious provider.

Jade

The roots of the jade clippings
have been growing since last August.
Almost a year, and they thick up the jars
as shocks of hair, clumps of mane. I found
the mother plant on a hillside, big body
drooping downward, her weight carving out
a cave of shade below.
She sang for me to harvest her.
I scooped her lengths and cut at the knuckles,
dropping swollen stems into the cup of my skirt.
I drove across town and stroked the petals until,
back in my kitchen, I gave each stalk wet residence.
I sat back to watch what life would make of itself.

An Overview of Summer Month by Month

June

As the first month of summer, June is partially a transition period and acts as the initial charge of the season. Typically, I start shifting my practice during this time, finding a good pause or resting place in whatever project I'm working on as I turn toward my social plans. This is also the month that I start to really feel grounded after the wild rush of spring. Coming out of the whirlwind of rebirth, I start to feel myself settle in for the coming months of leisure. In June, I tie up my loose ends so I can better lean into spontaneity.

Celebrating Summer Solstice

By the middle of June, summer takes hold fully and the Solstice is a perfect time to celebrate a complete entry into the sun season. This is a favorite holiday of mine because it roots me into my outward state of being, a turning point that brings me together with friends and family, excited to praise the rise of summer's character. Have a solstice party! Have a feast, a bonfire, a rowdy night of dancing and celebrating. Bring your people together and let the extroverted energy of summer take hold in an intentional way.

July

July is a great time to travel, a perfect moment to indulge in the big vibration of community that summer provides. Fulfill your plans, go on a road trip, perform in the park, visit your friends, do a short residency, and elaborate on what it is to connect with the outside world. This is the height of the season, a time when everyone is out and about, soaking up the sun, and relaxing and delighting in the wholeness of heat and togetherness.

August

A month of transition, when we might feel the first cool notes of fall, August is when we start settling down, but it's also when we get our last summer kicks. Take a moment for a final trip, luxuriate in the heat at the beach, spoil yourself with as much swimming and friend time as feasible, and begin to note the changes that you feel in these final weeks of the brightest season. I usually begin to tune my creative focus a bit in August, gently picking up my projects again as summer starts to wane.

Poems for Summer

"Summer" – John Ashbery

"June Wind" – Wendell Berry

"Strawberry Moon" – Franny Choi

"Summer Solstice" – Alex Dimitrov

"Evening Primrose" – Rita Dove

"To the Mulberry Tree" – Ross Gay

"A Strange New Cottage in Berkeley" – Allen Ginsberg

"Summer Night" – Louise Glück

"On Summer" – George Moses Horton

"Evening Sun" and "Philosophy in Warm Weather"
– Jane Kenyon

"Summer" – Robin Coste Lewis

"Living" – Denise Levertov

"Seasoning" – Audre Lorde

"Joy in the Woods" – Claude McKay

"Remembering Summer" and "Summer"
– W.S. Merwin

"August" and "The Summer Day" – Mary Oliver

"The Mountain Road Ends Here" – G. E. Patterson

"6/21" and "Holiday" – Adrienne Rich

"Finding Myself" – Ruth Stone

"Summer Solstice" – Jenny Zhang

How to Transition into Fall

Saying goodbye to summer is the hardest farewell that the seasons require, but fall is a lot of people's favorite time of year, so again, there's a balance. Be slow as you start to turn inward. Remember that you have three whole months to do the work of shifting from the external to the internal, so don't rush it. Steal any moments of summer that still exist and exalt the season of togetherness with as many gatherings as you can manage. Summer is so much fun, and turning from it can feel sad, but at the same time, it can be a relief after so much sun and socializing. Let it be both, and be sure to revel in it all as the days start getting shorter.

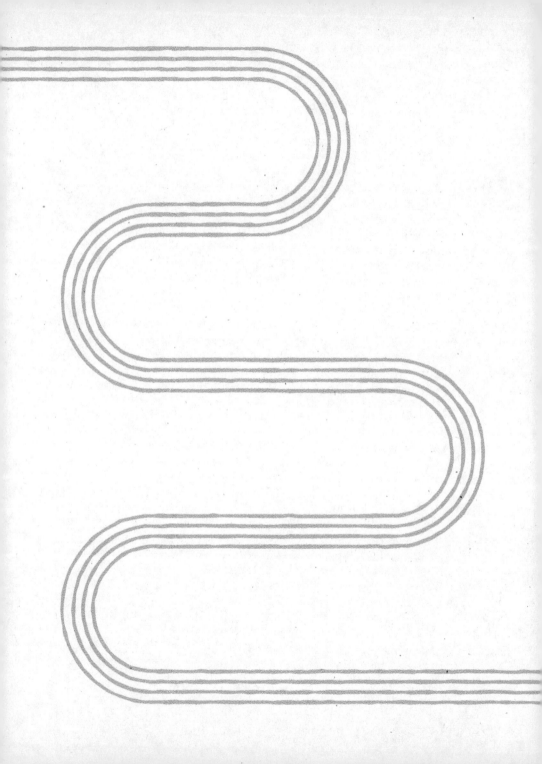

AUTUMN

Harvest – Gathering – Deceleration –
Clearing – Preparation – Stockpiling – Drying
– Transition – Contraction – Maturation –
Balance – Abundance – Nostalgia – Completion
– Activation – Melancholy – Cooling –
Discipline – Bounty – Preservation

***

How do we transition from outward to
inward and reap what we've sown?

Be like the squirrel and collect your reserves.
Be like the tree and shed all but your interior.

***

Autumn is many people's favorite time of year. The
feeling of this seasonal transition is crisp and exciting
for the senses, with an electric quality that fills the air for
the year's closing period of achievement and activity. It's a
time of great nostalgia, when we're still able to enjoy the
outdoors and children head back to school. Memories are
rampant, and gatherings are rich with traditional meals.

It's a balance point between inward and outward, when we put our sweaters on but aren't quite ready to close our doors completely.

After the rush of spring and the communal celebration of summer, autumn asks us to gradually turn back toward ourselves as we prepare for another winter of introspection. Some folks might be sad to leave behind the glory of summer and will need time to mourn the loss of its vibration. Others will be ready to leave behind the sunny months of extroversion and output. No matter how it feels to transition into fall, this is when we take inventory of all we've accomplished, notice what still needs to be tended to, and gather up our energy for a final push before the calendar year ends. This is the season that asks us to tie up loose ends, release all that doesn't serve us for the coming period of hibernation, and recognize our core needs after a long period of production and actualizing ideas. It's a time to take stock and ready ourselves for another deep dive into self-reflection.

The mainstays of fall are the harvest and preparation for winter. We spend the entire summer nurturing our creative ideas and bringing our designs and methods into fruition, and now we start the process of looking at the results, saving whatever still serves us, and culling that which is no longer needed. This season asks us to collect our reserves and prepare for the darker months. It's a systematic period that requires us to reignite our discipline so we're fully ready for the cold times ahead. How will our artistic efforts benefit from the greatness of winter if we don't adequately prepare for it? Now is the time to assemble the accumulated fruits of summer and preserve them for use during the coming stretch of solitude.

Autumn doesn't supply us with a lot of energy to start brand-new projects, but it does offer us a fresh surge of vivacity, asking us to observe and utilize all we've recently harvested from our explorations during the sunny seasons. Try to connect with the significant charge that arises during the fall months. Try to embrace this charge so you can finish up a few things before the year is complete. This autumnal buzz is what supports us in our frenetic time of gathering and conservation. We just have to be sure to focus as we downshift into it, saying goodbye to longer, warmer days.

Preparation

Note the metallic toll that vibrates in this final rush.

The crisp call of creation that urges
us to gather and arrange.

There is an electric spark that rises like a whip.

Its cold voice is pertinent and wise, preparing us to rest.

Fall speaks to us with certainty, stimulating
our last outpour of energy.

May we be robed in illumination, bending
low to collect what we need,

rising to the occasion of the harvest,
wide-eyed and ready.

With our skin still warm, we bow to the
beauty of earth's fine shadow.

It grows all around us with a smile
of abundance, reminding us

that we have time, we have the tools
for this closing composition,

for this conclusive song of bright instruction

that is both an ending and beginning.

Prompts from the Planet

What do plants and other animals do in the fall?

They gather their reserves of food, bury their stockpiles, and store their reinforcements.

Each creature knows the cold that's coming. They respond and harvest with swiftness.

The plants leave behind all reaching foliage. The core of each trunk is full and protected.

See how the nutrients are left for the health of the inner world?

The fungi rise into their fruiting bodies, getting ready for their wet wealth of winter rot.

Everything participates in preparation, honoring this final act of earth's profusion.

Remember, we are part of the same cycle.

Remember to ask yourself: *What is the natural world up to right now? How does it include me? How is it my mirror?*

PRACTICE: The Gratitude of Harvest

All throughout the fall, I find myself enlivened by the energy of the harvest. Whether it's just a resounding feeling of bounty or interactions with the fields that overflow with food, I return to a sense of endless gratitude again and again throughout the season. Fall is the best time to focus on what I'm thankful for, as the final offering of ripe crop and ready abundance reminds me to acknowledge all the work I've accomplished over the last few months of tending and buoying my personal practice.

My artistic customs feed me, my craft nourishes me, and so the harvest becomes a metaphor for all that I grow and collect beyond the farm and field. As the season begins to cool down, I ask myself what roots I want to dig up and preserve. What seeds are there to save? What considerations and experiences am I able to conserve that will carry me through the cold?

Ask yourself what you've finalized in the last six months that deserves celebration. Understand that even the smallest spark of inspiration is a seed, and if you take care of it now, give it attention, and bundle it up in a dry, dark, safe space, it can become its fullest form when the moment is right, after a period of rest and gestation. I carry around my ideas for books, songs, drawings, and performances for years, just as I carry around packets of seeds that I collect. I protect them all in a similar way and wait for the right moment to introduce them, when all the elements provide a ready atmosphere.

Before we move into the winter season of contemplation and creation, autumn helps us amass everything we'll need for our inward journey. How do we best acknowledge our creative concepts and inklings for future projects? In the last months of sun and outward energy, we continue to gather together. This is a time for ceremonial meals, where tables are set in praise of this final chapter of bounty, in gratitude for the soil, water, plants, and animals that give us so much. When we gather together to praise the worth of our work, witness the glorious changes that fall provides, and share in the electric feeling that infuses the air during these cooler months, we receive a sense of fullness that we can carry with us into winter.

As summer wanes and autumn takes hold, I often pick things from the garden or the farmers' market and make an altar where I can say my thanks and witness the vibrant bounty of the earth in one designated space. This is where I get myself focused and ready for the work of autumnal preparation. This season is really the last hurrah of unpressured togetherness before the wild rush of the holidays. I often place my altar as the centerpiece of a table, where I'll gather with friends and family to say goodbye to the season of warmth, to affirm the need for our connection in the coming months of darkness, and to lift our praise in unison so it's that much more resonant.

Coming together to celebrate the harvest is an old human tradition. It takes so many people to do the work of food collection and preservation, and it's the same with creative production as well. If we want to move into the quietness of snow with our minds clear and our bodies fully nourished, we need each other to complete the great tasks of accumulation and recognition. Sit down together and converse to mend any frayed bits of leftover creative objectives, tighten up the last of your artistic rambling ideas by sharing them, and rejoice in the warmth of communion before everyone holes up for winter.

This kind of shared acknowledgment and appreciation enriches my understanding of the natural world and the way it works with and without us. By showing thanks for this cycle of abundance, I recognize my place in it all, and this shines on my artistic practice as well. When I take the time to observe what I'm grateful for, I commit to a type of self-exploration. I focus on the harvest, not only to stockpile my creative ideas and record my summer adventures for future subject matter, but to affirm my place in the cosmic timeline. When I'm brimming with the gifts of summer, autumn gives me the space to recognize and praise this rich reality. Harvest time inspires me to figure out how I can best honor the gifts of the earth and show my gratitude for all I've received throughout the year.

Gratitude provides information about what inspires me. If I make a list of all the things I'm grateful for, especially at this time of year after so many wonderful outward experiences, I get to witness what moves me most, and that directly ties to potential subject matter for my creative efforts. I like to write about everything I'm thankful for so other folks can access the pieces and parts of life that ignite my artistic fire. There are many ways to approach and document gratitude, but list-making is my favorite method. Take some time to consider and write down everything that has filled you up so far this year. In this list, you'll likely find a surplus of material to use as you lean into the creative focus of the internal time that follows.

If you're feeling stuck, use the last bits of light as motivation.

Each season takes a while to really root in and flourish. As summer still speaks in the fall months, let these last gifts of sunshine energize you. Don't give in to the world of winter too soon. Fall can provide us with the exuberance to bring a finishing touch to many aspects of our practice. Let this spirit wash over you whenever you sense a hint of summer, whenever the cool air mixes perfectly with warm orange light, and know that sometimes all it takes is this act of noticing for the galvanizing spell of the season to hit you with a dose of its unique vigor.

Autumn Arrives

Wind moves the bay laurel leaves,
conducting a sound I imagine
porcupine quills make while rising,
or what I suppose
the raising of a dog's ruff
would sound like, if only we
could hear the gesture of fur.

I want to pinpoint the season's shift
if only to celebrate it properly.
Which birds stop trilling first?
Do certain plants sigh relief?

Summer gives its final
hours of warmth—saved for late
afternoon when I have given up
on sun. Suddenly the sky goes blue
with October's brightness.

Good tricks of light, nothing immediate—
all these starts
and stops to prepare me
for a pause,
a time of deep rest.

PRACTICE: Stockpiling & Preservation

As we celebrate the harvest with feasts and festivities, we also participate in the hard work of stockpiling everything we'll need for winter. Again, this aspect of seasonal nourishment applies not only to food reserves, but to artistic provisions as well.

Fall is an activated time when we make sure our creative spaces are cleared and ready for hibernation. Do you have all the materials, supplies, and notes you'll need? How will you preserve everything you've gathered from the last six months of growth and experience? Take stock of what you've collected and see if there's anything missing from your creative toolkit. We have our lists of gratitude, memories, and potential project notes. We have our full supply cabinets, our tuned and cared-for instruments, and our comfortable setups. These lists can be fairly short, but making sure we've tended to our visions and collected everything we need to dive deeper is a really important autumnal exercise.

Just like the food we seal up in cans and dehydrate so we can make use of it in the winter, the swirling bounty of inspiration and ideas that spring and summer supply us with must be cared for and organized so they don't go missing or become forgotten when it's time for us to go into our dens. This season is the last chance for us to pull anything we need from the outward world that will support us as we move into the next phase of inward work. I like to make a supply list to reference during autumn in order to make sure my studio space is ready for a winter of creative focus. The feeling of not having to leave my creative zone too often is comforting and energizing when it's cold outside. How can you best prepare for the upcoming period of focus and reverie?

ELEMENTAL INSTRUCTION: Metal

Autumn is connected to the element of metal. This is a drying time of year, a turn toward the cold, toward nostalgia and melancholy. Metal provides fortification, sturdiness, and structure.

Metal retains temperatures, holding heat or cold, responding and adapting to the season.

This is an ambitious element, and this energy is what enables us to prepare for winter.

In autumn, a specific persistence rises up in us. It's a reliable shine that ushers us onward into our final accomplishments for the year. Metal reminds us of our strength, that we have everything we need to build the foundation for our future practice. It returns us to the solid place of determination that resides in the heart of our creative process.

Are you open to the direction that metal brings? Can you allow yourself to adapt to the changing atmosphere with a balance of ease and resilience? In what areas of your artistry can you emphasize finesse and control? Are you able to be both soft and hard at once? Let the determined character of metal show you how to embrace your perseverance as you formulate and secure your winter intentions.

If you're feeling stuck, remember to regulate.

As fall begins and temperatures waver from warm to cool, it's important to remember that physical and emotional regulation isn't always easy. Regulation might seem like something that's just related to the body, but the way you interact with the undulating energy of fall will affect your creative practice as well. In order to tune in to what we need, whether it's a little bit of communal summer energy or a dose of autumnal nourishment, we have to be in conversation with our necessary adjustments. As such, regulation requires heightened presence and awareness.

In this transitional season, our mood can be unpredictable and a lot of emotion can arise. Many of us experience seasonal depression that begins in fall. If we make space in our creative practice to include our response to the changing weather, we can tend to ourselves accordingly. Sometimes I'm not able to follow the quick shifts in temperature and keep my attitude in sync with the start and stop of autumn. As our summers become hotter and longer, it will take more preparation for us to interact with this sporadic seasonal shift. I know I'm greatly affected by temperature, so I do a lot of careful arranging to regulate and settle into my creative discipline, even if the cold doesn't come as soon as I'd like.

How do you respond to this aspect of the changing season? Are you familiar with your needs around emotional and physical regulation? Are there tools you can use to find a balance and take care of yourself in the drastic ups and downs that autumn instigates? Try setting some intentions as you prepare for this undulation. Be sure to check in with yourself and see what rituals and responses you can practice when the fall transition becomes uncomfortable.

PRACTICE: Make a Pilgrimage

This is the time for migration, when so many animals make their yearly move to warmer climates. For many creatives, the desire to travel fits into any season, as it usually offers fresh insight and innovation. Getting out of your routine and opening up to new experiences is an age-old way to invite in a new Muse or shift your creative energy. It's important to note, though, that not every trip is a pilgrimage.

There are places that I visit again and again, spiritual spots that recharge me, areas that are meaningful to my personal mythology, that I return to because they energize me beyond what vacation or relaxation can offer. Visiting these places is a ritual that renews my poetic mindset. My creative work speaks of these landscapes, pulling from them as if from a deep well, and each visit enriches my practice by adding to my stories and traditions.

Is there a journey that you continually make or would like to make to a place you respect? Somewhere that lifts your spirit or realigns you with the source of your inspiration? Autumn is a wonderful time to make this type of journey.

A pilgrimage can ready us for winter, and it can help us align with the wellspring of our practice. Many people make it a priority to go somewhere during fall to see the leaves change color. This is a pilgrimage that connects them to the transitional nature of autumn. When we take ourselves out of our day-to-day space in order to pay homage to the shifting season, we can better reap the benefits, which often means fully appreciating the unique beauty autumn showcases. It may seem like a simple act, but this effort has the potential to root you into the lessons that this time of year is known for, and it can help slow you down as you begin the significant transition into coolness and dryness.

I continuously visit a bigleaf maple tree that I have a sacred relationship with, and I love making this trip in the fall because I get to see the fullness of its transformation. Witnessing my tree change allows me to better appreciate earth's complexity and find myself akin to this transition. If you're unable to travel and see the leaves turn, maybe you can find a creative way to engage with this metamorphosis. Turn to the plants in your neighborhood. Find a big tree in the park that you can visit again and again as it changes. How are the plants marking this important adjustment before the cold comes to land? Let them be your reminder that turning inward is a process that happens gradually. Let them lead you into your own altered rhythm with gentleness and a beautiful palette. The following poem is about my maple tree. I try to make a yearly pilgrimage to visit it, and this always ignites inspiration or provides affirmation in my poetic process.

Perciple

The wolf boy led me to you in fall
and by winter he'd moved on
to younger flesh. I started
coming back alone. Following
the cut of soil woven through
snowberries, I'd round the corner
and cry. A swollen temple of forty trunks,
you contained it all—a kitchen, a closet,
an altar, and most importantly
a bedroom where my body fit
in a slot with moss, a narrow casket.
I brought an offering each time,
filled your cup with crystals,
bobby pins and buttons.
I slept inside of you, wrapped
in a sleeping bag and tarp, reading
Whitman, eating soup from a thermos,
and rubbing myself. It wasn't until
spring that you told me your name.
I started licking bark, kissing roots,
collecting samaras, those winged seeds
that aided my angelic belief.
I drew symbols on your naked stag

with a ballpoint pen and wrapped
a colored sash there, as high
as I could climb. We were married
when your leaves were green,
my emblem of the earth, this place
my greatest love. I found a few notes
stuffed into a hole, signs of others
who adored your throne.
That's okay, I have others, too, but no
human could be you. If I marry
a person, the ritual will start here.
We'll kneel for permission and bow
into the taste of soil. Once I encircled you
with fallen sticks, wept and bled
at your feet. Now I see you changing.
Your limbs age with every visit, on each
pilgrimage I find the weight of time
revealing itself, sagging boughs, the entire
kitchen broken into rot. You don't need
a singular body to be my spouse. We protect
each other from afar, even as we're dying,
my husband, my wife, my god.
My one and only maple.

Transition

Witness how gravity works with the
trees as they shed their leaves.

What's willing to drift away will let
loose in this timely withdrawal.

We gather up our goodness in abundant
fields, with feasts of gratitude.

Moving toward balance, we alight with
a final surge of maturation.

Thankful for our season of sun, we dull
our colors, readying for sleep.

Coolness clears us and we close up a bit.

May we not be afraid of ending, but
thrilled by this beginning.

The coming death of winter is also incubation for rebirth.

May we delight in this equitable exchange.

Reflecting upon our growth, we
contract for the coming snow.

Stepping outside once more, we breathe
deep to ignite our finishing flame.

PRACTICE: Reflecting on Growth

One of the most potent aspects of fall is the feeling of nostalgia that strikes when the season shifts. There are various reasons for this overwhelming sense of remembrance that comes with crisp air, pumpkin patches, and corn mazes. For many people, autumn is culturally linked to childhood, the return to school, and shared traditions, which set these few months apart from the rest.

In such a sentimental period, I like to take stock of my personal growth and note what I've accomplished over the year. Balanced alongside my youthful memories, this reflection on who I am today gives me an interesting life overview. I get to indulge in feelings from the past while considering how much I've changed.

This brush with nostalgia easily gets existential as I consider what memory even is and how it affects my current understanding of self. When I look closely at everything that's happened in my life, I often find inspiration; the Muse of the past comes knocking, and I'm urged to use this calling as impetus for creative process.

Nostalgia can be really strange and off-putting, but it can also act as a source of artistry. It's often the haunting pain of the past or an experience that leaves us yearning that incites our creative response, if only to find some sense of healing or transformation in it. The feeling of fall can conjure up an outlet like this, and if we're willing to utilize it, we may end up with a lot of creative fuel.

Here are some questions to help prompt a fruitful exploration of nostalgic inspiration with an emphasis on growth and transformation.

- What is something you've let go of in the last year of your life, and how has your life changed because of it?

- What is something that you've wished for but haven't yet received?

- Write about what comes up when you contemplate growing old.

- What is one thing you simply must do before you die?

- What are you most curious about in your current life?

- Take an inventory of your skills. Be sure to include everything, like your listening skills, for example, not just the tactile or quantitative.

- What is something that you've consistently sacrificed throughout your life, and why do you do this?

- Think as far back as possible to your very first memory and write it down in as much detail as you can.

- Set a timer for ten minutes and try to make a quick timeline of your life. What shows up in this overview? Is there anything here that you'd like to examine further? Do any of these significant moments inspire you to create something in response?

I often write about past experiences, as they affect the present moment, and autumn feels like a great occasion for this kind of work. Nostalgia touches every artistic medium, so this is as fine a time as ever to lean into the odd nature of wistfulness and let it serve your practice.

Sometimes remembrance is too much, and I intuitively know whether or not it's the right time to go down memory lane. This exploration of the past can either be a whirlwind of emotion or extremely affirmative. It can also serve as an interesting inspection of the human mind, how memory actually works, and the various ways we approach our stores of former experience. Take care of yourself in this process of uncovering, but if you're able to welcome the insights that arise when the air cools down and the scent of dried leaves floats on the wind, you might reveal an abundance of material to pull from for your practice. Here's an example of a poem of mine that speaks on past experience and the way it can take new shape as time keeps moving forward.

Not Haunted

I thought you were in love
with your mother. I remember
a dragonfly on your brother's lip.
I remember biting your chest
so hard I saw stars.
Instead of growing up and opening
a school together, you decided
to become a doctor and I left you
for a maniac who hopped trains.
There was never anyone
better than you, eyes like crystal,
radical breast bone, a question
always living on your tongue.
I thought you'd haunt me for years.

You became a Buddhist and I rode
my bicycle through the streets
of New Orleans to meet you
and your new girlfriend.
On the way I ripped my pants,
the cuff caught in the chain.
The three of us swam naked in the pool
and I finally stopped wanting you.
This girl was much softer than I'd ever be.
Finally far enough away from your home,
I thought about your mother's strong
arms, her critical gaze, and realized
that I was the one most like her,
and you were not in love.

If you're feeling stuck, ask yourself, *What is time?*

Autumn is the season that sinks me into my most uninhibited questions about time. In spring, I'm too caught up in the enormous rush of beauty to really tap into any solid understanding of time, but in fall there's an obvious, gradual, surface-level shift that I witness day by day, and this instigates my deep consideration of time. The days start getting shorter, many of us set our clocks back, and although this shift might seem subtle, it can have a direct impact on our mood and creative output.

To comprehend the passing of time throughout the year, I have to keep a close eye on at least two physical calendars, one handwritten and one on the computer. Time management is at the heart of discipline, and I've finely tuned this part of my practice to be utilitarian, but in fall I let myself slip into nostalgia and memories, musing on the past, causing a somewhat existential review of what I imagine time to be. It's a construct, of course, so I know I can reimagine it over and over again as I live a life of awareness and curiosity.

Give yourself the opportunity to wonder over and research time and memory—the way it plays into every aspect of our lives, how it informs our practices and creative projects. Take a moment to consider how the passing of time influences the way you create, altering how you bring your visions into the world and when. Time touches every part of our lives, and fall gives us the chance to reconfigure how we approach it. Witness how it feels to lean into nostalgia. Can you write about your understanding of time to widen your perspective and rearrange your strategy when it comes to managing it?

PRACTICE: Connecting with Color

No matter what your artistic genre is, color provides us all with mysterious and sensual information. Spring bursts with vibrant hues, and summer expresses the entire, saturated spectrum, but something about the palette of fall connects me with color in a deeper way.

Autumn presents us with the last push of pastels and rich tones that give character to entropy as the plant world begins its process of shedding before resting. This is when color begins its yearly exit, and it goes out with a fantastic show. Goldenrod bursts with plumes of yellow. Oak leaves dull their green gift and fade into many versions of orange. Every expression of color starts to soften in fall, and this agreeable wash of pigment eases me into my exploration of all the possible tints. It's almost as if these less-showy shades inspire me to exhale and then, in my state of ease, I can think about color in a more expansive way.

In other seasons, color can be overwhelming for me to approach with my queries and considerations. In spring it engulfs me in a state of awe and bliss; in summer it floods me with joyous overload; but in fall I can really get to the root of my complete interest in color without feeling delirious in it. I'm intrigued by the endless stimulation that color rouses in me, and I continuously muse on all the ways it impacts my practice. Autumn allows for my full appreciation as I experience the spectrum in its final push, a fleeting moment that gives me one last chance to indulge in this phenomenon.

As I write this in mid-September, I have just started writing poems about colors with my friend Mo Neuharth. It's incredible how much comes up when we give ourselves the space to delve into each pigment. How does color appear in your practice? See how many things it touches, how much reaction it causes, how significant it is in the details that make up each experience. What emotions are connected to the colors you witness now? Does a certain color bring you comfort? Do the changing colors of fall bring you even further into nostalgia? What information does each tint offer? As you enjoy the presence of autumnal colors, give each tone some time, name the ones that draw you in, describe them, explore them, and let this finishing act be celebrated through your awe and recognition. Here is a poem about the way the color yellow once helped me find balance on the edge between summer and fall.

Yellow

Last week, I threw an old
yellow apple out my cabin window,
directly into the throne of a mighty sword fern.
Now I no longer see its color caught
in the afternoon light. In a matter of days,
the sun has fallen below my tree line.
This means shadow lasts longer—
dawn is not a bright shimmer
but a light shade of blue-grey.

Yet, the folks who own the meadow
are still enjoying summer. Their season
just across the valley is different than mine.
Even now they continue to soak
tea bags in the early rays, water
changing to amber in a glass pitcher.

Still, the sunflower
in the garden has turned
toward my house. Its tawny face
is the first thing I see after
I lose sight of the apple—
a last symbol of warmth
before the darkness of fall settles.

PRACTICE: When the Veil Is Thin

As I continue to reference and emphasize the potent energy of fall, it's important to also mention the magical and melancholic quality of the season. I'm no aficionado on the spooky nature of this time of year, but culturally there are many aspects of autumn that provide us with strangeness and oddities. It's also the time in our seasonal cycle that brings about death and decomposition. With our surroundings moving toward an ending, we're closer in many ways to the closure that exists for all of us, and this brings into focus otherworldly sensations and eerie mythologies, which can give us a lot of creative input.

Death offers us so much imaginative fuel. Some of us shy away from it and its mournful qualities, but many artists embrace the morose and morbid. If there's a moment in the year that allows us to collectively connect with the energy and intrigue of death, it's fall. Instead of the obvious and silent aspects of death that exist during winter, autumn is the moment that precedes the end. It grazes it and connects with closure while life still clings around us.

Various cultures lean into this phase, celebrating the dead, communicating with spirits, and openly acknowledging the unknown. This shared brush with the afterlife, with ghosts and ghouls, is great fodder for creative thought. There's an inextinguishable interest in the type of uncanny query that this season inspires, with theories and ancient tales that support an often playful and very real fascination with all of the mystery that surfaces during autumn.

- How does this affect your practice?

- Can you tap into the lure and lore of all that exists beyond the veil?

- Does this energy interest you in any way?

- Do you embrace death or fear it?

- Do you think of death as an ending or a beginning?

- Does melancholy inspire you or bring you down?

- Are you mourning the loss of summer or indulging in the gifts of fall?

Knowing where you are with all of this will help you find your fulcrum in fall, and this balance will undoubtedly permeate into your practice. I enjoy this feeling that fall provides. It excites me to brush up against entropy, and the ending of the outward seasons holds a promise of gestation for my practice. A lot of my work involves listening to the world around me, but I'm also deeply fascinated by all that exists beyond my sight in the unknown presence swirling in and out of my everyday experience. Fall gives me the space to delight in the supernatural and the thrill of all that resides in the balance between life and death. In the following poem, I explore a moment I had with a supernatural presence. You can see how my openness allowed me to delve into the imaginative possibility inspired by such an unusual experience.

Mavi

The very first time I slept in my cabin,
I fell into dreams immediately.
Before my eyes closed, I saw nothing
but a thick mass of black.

I awoke in the night to find
someone at the end of my bed.
White outline, floating form,
not human, but star stuff
and certainly there.

I said aloud with ease a word I did not know:
Mavi
then sleep came again.

In the morning I ran down the trail
toward the lodge and came to a halt
at the foot of a bending bay laurel.

Inhaling the pepper sweet smell, I noticed
rot by the roots, white dust
mixing with black soil.

Good guide, who halted me in this land
of green wonder. My protector.

I touched its necklike trunk, its snaking body,
and said it again:
Mavi

PRACTICE: Clearing

After the shedding that summer necessitates, fall takes hold with its windy weather and dropping leaves, clearing us of anything heavy that we don't need for winter.

Depending on where you live, this will be the season that returns us to the need for fire. There might be celebratory bonfires in spring, wildfires may rage with regenerative purpose in summer, but in autumn the element of fire is more utilitarian as we return to our physical need for heat.

There's nothing like the smell of smoke in the air to remind me of clearing and complete renewal. What can you throw into the flames that isn't essential for your progression or creative advancement? Now is the time to start loosening your grip on the countless tendrils of summer expression, keeping close only what excites you most.

There's a sensual reset that happens this time of year as we start the process of cooling down. Clearing our practice of the fiery feeling of summer is a gradual process that begins when the temperature starts dropping. Our meals change, our clothes get thicker, and we open ourselves to the autumnal routine of clearing our schedules and altering our focus.

Fall helps me return to my acute observation, letting the immensity of the outside world begin to fade away, while all of the smallest and more personal details rise into view. It's as if I'm harvesting only the finest aspects of the crop, the bits and pieces of the surrounding world that supply me with the most intrigue and inspiration. Here is a poem that exemplifies the shift in perspective that autumn reveals.

Like a Pearl

Miso soup for breakfast

because fall chill

is suddenly here.

A handful of kombu

from the last harvest

and a purple carrot from the garden.

I bite down on a small

black snail

and hold it up to the light,

its perfect spiral shape preserved.

What are you willing to bring with you into the depths of introspection? Is there a clearing ritual that you enjoy or one that you might research and employ during this time? Perhaps you need to create a ceremony that ushers you through the grief that sometimes arises when we say goodbye to summer?

Think of what happens when all the dead leaves are forgotten and left on the surface of the grass. They decompose and create soil as they smother the soft green blades. This is the season of choices. What will we remove, and what will we nurture in order to safeguard all we'd like to continue witnessing in growth and wholeness once the snow melts? Do you have ideas that you need to bag up, document, or burn before the sleepy season of winter asks you to put everything down and rest? Give yourself the opportunity to clear away anything that isn't calling your name. If you can't choose what's worthwhile and what isn't, storage is possible, and in the cold so many things keep well even without much attention.

Autumnal endeavors are typically lit by the exuberance of preparation, which facilitates a period of tending to anything that might block us from our readiness for winter. Even the fresh air of fall clears our lungs, and with this we become unhindered, open, and excited in this season that readies us for the coming lull.

PRACTICE: Closure

One of the most invigorating aspects of fall is the way it provides us with the impetus for completion. The other day I was speaking with my friend Nicole Disson, who expressed that, as the year begins to wane, she feels inclined to clarify a single creative pursuit she'd like to accomplish before the end of the cycle. This is not the same as making a full summer schedule, rather it's more intentional and focused on a finale that will satisfy the need for fulfillment.

The electricity that fills the air in autumn can serve as a charge for us to finalize a project or plan a closing performance. It's an opportunity for resolution so when we move into our darker dens, we don't carry the weight of unfinished tasks with us.

Try choosing one thing you'd like to complete before autumn is over—a final edit, some last tweaks of lyrics or brushstrokes, a demo recording, or an intimate harvest concert. Choose a creative task that you know you can finish, and let the rush of fall guide you through this conclusion.

Closure is the sibling of clearing; the two go hand in hand. So when we work through our rituals of release, tuning in to cleansing smoke and tiny details, we're also preparing to finish our outward offerings so we can wholly turn inward. This shift of focus requires a sense of cessation, and the best way to secure this is to dedicate yourself to something you can complete before the first sign of snow.

An Overview of Fall Month by Month

September

During this month we fluctuate between summer and fall with waves of heat and surprisingly cool nights. The start and stop of September should be met with compassion as we gradually collect our layers, plan our final outings, and rejoice in the greatness of the harvest. This is when I start shifting into the excitement of fall, waking up from the relaxing dream of summer, and finding a new spark to propel me into one last burst of action.

Celebrating the Autumnal Equinox

This is our moment of balance, when we straddle the space between summer's brightness and winter's darkness. Autumn is our middle ground, and the equinox provides us with a reason to celebrate this equilibrium. This might be a moment for internal evaluation as you calculate your needs and energy reserves, or you might use this time as the ultimate celebration, gathering with friends to say goodbye to summer while practicing rituals to welcome the spirit of fall.

October

As October arrives, we've regulated a bit more, feeling our way into coolness, deciphering the gifts of the harvest, and finding the fulcrum of the season. This is the month when the cycle of death really sets in, the veil is thin, and the growing world begins to completely shut down.

There's still that bright spark in the air as the trees make their closing remarks with dried leaves and bare branches, and so there's still time to revel in the outdoors before the cold comes.

November

The fullness of fall is here, winter is standing in the shadow, and we are wise to wrap up whatever needs tending before we enter our dens. This is the last hurrah, a time for family visits, storytelling, and hearty meals that will fill us up for the inward journey to come. In November we make time for our last acts of closure and clearing.

Poems for Fall

"An Autumn Burning" and "September 2, 1969"
– Wendell Berry

"September" – Raymond Carver

"the lesson of falling leaves" – Lucille Clifton

"November for Beginners" – Rita Dove

"To the Fig Tree on 9th and Christian" – Ross Gay

"Autumnal" and "Burning Leaves" – Louise Glück

"Watching Blackbirds Turn to Ghosts"
– Rachel Eliza Griffiths

"Autumn" – Ursula K. Le Guin

"Fall Song" – Joy Harjo

"Ripeness" – Jane Hirshfield

"The Tree of Fire" – Ada Limón

"October" and "Return" – Audre Lorde

"Leaves" – Derek Mahon

"First Thanksgiving" – Sharon Olds

"September" – Grace Paley

"November 1968" – Adrienne Rich

"Autumn Day" – Rainer Maria Rilke

"September Songs" – Reginald Shepherd

"Thanksgiving 2006" – Ocean Vuong

How to Transition into Winter

As with any other seasonal shift, don't rush into your quiet, warm winter space. Give fall the respect it deserves as the season that offers us a finishing push of creative enthusiasm. Take pause to slowly uncover any new ideas that will buoy you in the following months. Gather together, collect everything you need, double-check your lists of requirements, and look over your shoulder for a long time before tightening your scarf and pulling your door closed.

CONCLUSION

At the end of the classic 1990s film *FernGully*, the fairy-witch Crysta goes to change the newly enlightened Zak back into his appropriate human size so he can return to society and help stop the destruction of the rainforest.

Before she enacts this shape-shifting magic, she says to him, "Remember everything."

She means remember everything that just happened to you in the rainforest, every life-altering experience, every moment of transformation and inspiration, every heart-expanding connection, every incredible creature, and every earth-powered lesson. Remember it all and take it back to your world, share it with your fellow humans, and put an end to the needless decimation of our glorious planet.

But Crysta knows how forgetful we are.

As soon as Zak is back in his big human body, he meets up with his fellow loggers and they start walking back to the city, chuckling, as Zak says, "Guys, we have a lot of work to do." Crysta can see in this moment that he is already forgetting.

So she gives one last bold display, one more push for remembrance: she makes the twisted tree that encases the evil spirit of pollution and greed bloom with thousands of pink flowers. It's bold magic, it's striking, and she hopes it will be memorable enough to inspire Zak to hold on to all he's learned. Maybe. Maybe not.

He and the loggers do stop, awestruck, staring at the blooming tree. They need to return home and brew up a plan that will make a difference, that will alter the current system. Crysta can only hope her gesture will be enough to encourage real change back in the human world.

Like Zak, we need help remembering. We need guidance in order to find the path forward. We require assistance in bringing our brief moments of clarity into long-lasting actualization. We do nothing of the sort all on our own.

The act of creation takes practice, dedication, a schedule of sorts, or at the very least a committed rhythm. The earth provides this for us. The purpose of this book is to remind you that the seasons offer an inherent pattern of contraction and expansion for creative energy. You don't need to reinvent the wheel or struggle internally to develop a perfect system for artistic discipline, because the seasons will show you the way. My hope is that my examples of seasonal practice and ritual will help you align your personal process with the phases of sun and shadow.

Our creative practice is part of the natural cycle. It's what makes our world. May we all move according to the cadence of where we live. May each landscape and season show us with weather, temperature, and disposition when to turn inward and when to change direction. May we remember to listen to everything the earth teaches and trust it to lead us onward in our efforts of expression and growth.

ACKNOWLEDGMENTS

First and foremost, I offer my gratitude to the earth, my ever-loving guide, this perfect planet that gives and gives and gives. To all the spirits of the land, the protectors of place, the people who steward and care for our home, this is for you.

My heartfelt thanks to my agent Kate Woodrow and my team at Sounds True for making sure this project got its chance to thrive. To Diana Ventimiglia and Lyric Dodson for your editing eyes and careful considerations. To my longtime editor and dear friend, Matthew Phipps, thank you for being with me through it all.

Eric Johnson, my love, thank you for your incredible attention and support as I worked on this book season after season. You always made me feel so sure of myself, even when I was wandering in the park listening to the oaks or on the floor surrounded by books and papers. I love you the most, my one and only.

Hallie Bateman, you are my champion, my go-to for creative conversation, and this book really came into the world by way of your love and support. Thank you for always being down to share inspiration and dream huge dreams with me. You are a rare gift, and I know we'll lift each other up for the rest of our silly, artful lives.

Rachel Zingoni, my spiritual partner in earth worship, I thought of you the entire time I worked on this book and am so grateful for your enthusiasm. Sharing our spiritual practice continues to be a grounding point for me throughout all the seasons of my life.

Marlee Grace, my soulmate in the creative work of book-making and earth-loving, thank you for the introduction that got me to this point on the timeline where this book is possible. I'm so grateful for and deeply wowed by our endless connection.

Meredith Clark, your grace and wisdom is always with me, so it's within these pages as well. Thank you for being the very best. Truly.

Everyone at Folklife Farm—Peter Barker, Taja, Cindy, and Larry—thank you for giving me the time and space to nurture this idea when it was in its infancy. It all started under the gaze of the madrone trees, looking over that glorious valley, where my life transformed. I can't thank you enough.

Shelby Duncan, thank you for always checking in, sharing your appreciation, and believing in me. The way you witness my passion is the deepest affirmation. I will love you forever.

Nicole Disson, Lady of the Mountain, thank you for your reflections and for our endless shared excitement over the land we love. I get so much joy imagining you reading these pages, smiling, and seeing yourself in the details we both revere.

Thank you to Natalie Ross for all of our inspiring conversations, but especially for connecting the words *imagination* and *intuition* in my spiritual vocabulary.

I'm grateful to my dear friends in Detroit who have listened to me talk about this project with great attention for the last year, especially Melissa Drasby, Mo Neuharth, and Rosemary Brown. Whether you're taking me to an amazing trail in the woods or talking to me about cover design, your friendship is crucial. It's an honor to share my life with you, and I appreciate each of you entirely.

POEM SOURCES

"All Nature" first appeared in *The Edge of the Continent Volume Two: The City* (Rare Bird Books, 2019).

"No Seasons" first appeared in *The Edge of the Continent Volume Two: The City* (Rare Bird Books, 2019).

"Only Water Helps" first appeared in *The Edge of the Continent Volume Two: The City* (Rare Bird Books, 2019).

"The Whale Dream" first appeared in *The Edge of the Continent Volume Three: The Desert* (Rare Bird Books, 2020).

"Desert Bear" first appeared in *The Edge of the Continent Volume Three: The Desert* (Rare Bird Books, 2020).

"The Great Valley of Myself" first appeared in *The Edge of the Continent Volume Three: The Desert* (Rare Bird Books, 2020).

"Spring" first appeared in *The Edge of the Continent Volume Three: The Desert* (Rare Bird Books, 2020).

"The Chosen One" first appeared in *The Edge of the Continent Volume Two: The City* (Rare Bird Books, 2019).

"Datura" first appeared in *The Edge of the Continent Volume Two: The City* (Rare Bird Books, 2019).

"The Overgrown Cul-de-sac" first appeared in *The Edge of the Continent Volume Two: The City* (Rare Bird Books, 2019).

"A Morning" first appeared in *The Edge of the Continent Volume Three: The Desert* (Rare Bird Books, 2020).

"Devil's Elbow" first appeared in *The Edge of the Continent Volume One: The Forest* (Rare Bird Books, 2018).

"The Work That Cannot Be Done Alone" first appeared in *Help in the Dark Season: Poems* (Write Bloody Publishing, 2019).

"My God Comes to Me" *The Edge of the Continent Volume One: The Forest* (Rare Bird Books, 2018).

"I Live in the Woods" *The Edge of the Continent Volume One: The Forest* (Rare Bird Books, 2018).

"Nothing Will End" first appeared in *The Edge of the Continent Volume Two: The City* (Rare Bird Books, 2019).

"I Call the Sun Umalet" *The Edge of the Continent Volume One: The Forest* (Rare Bird Books, 2018).

"Staying with Angela" first appeared in *The Edge of the Continent Volume Three: The Desert* (Rare Bird Books, 2020).

"Midwives of Newborn Symbology" *The Edge of the Continent Volume One: The Forest* (Rare Bird Books, 2018).

"Jade" first appeared in *The Edge of the Continent Volume Two: The City* (Rare Bird Books, 2019).

"Autumn Arrives" first appeared in *The Edge of the Continent Volume One: The Forest* (Rare Bird Books, 2018).

"Perciple" first appeared in *Help in the Dark Season: Poems* (Write Bloody Publishing, 2019).

"Not Haunted" first appeared in *Help in the Dark Season: Poems* (Write Bloody Publishing, 2019).

"Yellow" first appeared in *The Edge of the Continent Volume One: The Forest* (Rare Bird Books, 2018).

"Mavi" first appeared in *The Edge of the Continent Volume One: The Forest* (Rare Bird Books, 2018).

"Like a Pearl" first appeared in *The Edge of the Continent Volume One: The Forest* (Rare Bird Books, 2018).

ABOUT
SOUNDS TRUE

Sounds True was founded in 1985 by Tami Simon with a clear mission: to disseminate spiritual wisdom. Since starting out as a project with one woman and her tape recorder, we have grown into a multimedia publishing company with a catalog of more than 3,000 titles by some of the leading teachers and visionaries of our time, and an ever-expanding family of beloved customers from across the world.

In more than three decades of evolution, Sounds True has maintained its focus on our overriding purpose and mission: to wake up the world. We offer books, audio programs, online learning experiences, and in-person events to support your personal growth and awakening, and to unlock our greatest human capacities to love and serve.

At SoundsTrue.com you'll find a wealth of resources to enrich your journey, including our weekly Insights at the Edge podcast, free downloads, and information about our nonprofit Sounds True Foundation, where we strive to remove financial barriers to the materials we publish through scholarships and donations worldwide.

To learn more, please visit SoundsTrue.com/freegifts or call us toll-free at 800.333.9185.

Together, we can wake up the world.

sounds true
WAKING UP THE WORLD

ABOUT THE
AUTHOR

Jacqueline Suskin is a poet and educator who has been teaching workshops, writing books, and creating spontaneous poetry around the world since 2009. She has composed more than 40,000 improvisational poems with her ongoing writing project, Poem Store. Suskin is the author of eight books, including *The Edge of the Continent* (volumes 1–3), *Help in the Dark Season*, and *Every Day Is a Poem*. Her work has been featured in various publications including the *New York Times*, the *Atlantic*, and *Yes!* magazine. As the Artist in Residence at Folklife Farm from 2019 to 2021, Suskin founded a retreat program and continues to host artists from around the world. She lives in Detroit where she works as a teaching artist with InsideOut Literary Arts, bringing nature poetry into classrooms.